THE

LATTER-DAY SAINTS'

EMIGRANTS' GUIDE

THE

LATTER-DAY SAINTS'

EMIGRANTS' GUIDE:

BEING A

TABLE OF DISTANCES,

SHOWING ALL THE

SPRINGS, CREEKS, RIVERS, HILLS, MOUNTAINS,
CAMPING PLACES, AND ALL OTHER NOTABLE PLACES,

FROM COUNCIL BLUFFS,

TO THE

VALLEY OF THE GREAT SALT LAKE.

ALSO, THE

LATITUDES, LONGITUDES AND ALTITUDES
OF THE PROMINENT POINTS ON THE ROUTE.

TOGETHER WITH REMARKS ON THE NATURE OF THE LAND,
TIMBER, GRASS, &c.

THE WHOLE ROUTE HAVING BEEN CAREFULLY MEASURED BY A ROADOME-
TER, AND THE DISTANCE FROM POINT TO POINT, IN
ENGLISH MILES, ACCURATELY SHOWN.

BY W. CLAYTON.

ST. LOUIS:

MO. REPUBLICAN STEAM POWER PRESS—CHAMBERS & KNAPP,
1848.

EDITED BY STANLEY B. KIMBALL

WITH A BIOGRAPHICAL INTRODUCTION BY JAMES B. ALLEN

THE PATRICE PRESS/1983

Library of Congress
Cataloging in Publication Data

Clayton, William, 1814-1879.
　The Latter-day Saints' emigrants' guide.
　Originally published: St. Louis : Mo. Repub-
lican Steam Power Press, 1848.
　Includes index.
　1. West (U.S.) — Description and travel —
1848-1860 — Guide-books. 2. West (U.S.) —
Distances, etc.
I. Kimball, Stanley Buchholz. II. Allen,
James B. III. Title. IV Title: Emigrants' guide.
F593.C63　1983　　917.8'042　　83-2473
ISBN 0-935284-27-3

Published by
The Patrice Press
1701 South Eighth Street / St. Louis MO 63104

Printed in the United States of America

CONTENTS

William Clayton

THE LATTER-DAY SAINTS' EMIGRANTS' GUIDE:
HOW & WHY IT CAME TO BE

BY JAMES B. ALLEN

I T WAS A COLD DAY in February 1846 when William Clayton suddenly found himself among the first of thousands of Mormons to be forced from their homes in Nauvoo, Illinois. Such was the tragic beginning of an epic pioneer adventure, but it was not long before this English immigrant made several important contributions to the history and imagery of Western America: "Come, Come Ye Saints," perhaps the most poignant and well known of all Mormon hymns; *William Clayton's Journal,* one of the finest firsthand accounts available of the memorable crossing of the plains by the vanguard company of Mormon pioneers; and *The Latter-day Saints' Emigrants' Guide,* the most important guide available for the pioneers who followed him and one of the significant sources for guidebooks created for other westering Americans in the mid-nineteenth century.

Though he was never a top Church leader, since early 1842 William Clayton had been deeply involved in almost every important development in the Church of Jesus Christ of Latter-day Saints. As Joseph Smith's personal scribe and confidant, he was privy to the beginnings of several innovations that eventually came to characterize Mormonism, including plural marriage and the sacred temple ceremonies. After the death of the founding prophet, Clayton continued in his duties under the new leader, Brigham Young. Among other things, he was responsible for many of the public and private records of the Church. As clerk of the semi-secret but highly influential "Council of Fifty," he was in on the actual planning of the western migration, and because of his well-known skills as a scribe and record keeper, Brigham Young insisted that he be among the first to leave Nauvoo as well as become a member of the vanguard company that led the way to the Salt Lake Valley.

By the fall of 1845, the Mormons knew they must vacate Nauvoo soon or be driven out by their enemies. Mob activity was mounting, and there was little hope for help either from the state or the national government. Brigham Young finally promised they would leave in the spring, which provided some respite, but that meant the Mormons had only six months to organize emigrant companies, build wagons, gather provisions for the hard months ahead, sell their property, and make all the other preparations for transferring their society to the Far West. In the meantime, local pressures began building again, and on February 2, 1846, Church leaders decided that some of them, at least, must leave immediately. The cold and bitter exodus was helped only by the fact that on a few days the Mississippi River froze over so they could take their wagons and animals across on ice instead of flatboats.

William Clayton's preparations were probably more hectic and frustrating than most. He had to settle many of the financial affairs of the Church, work on land records, take care of a myriad of miscellaneous bookkeeping matters, pack all the records for transportation across the plains, and do all this while he was ill. In addition, he had several wives and children for whom he had to find provisions, transportation and shelter. When he finally departed Nauvoo on February 27 he left behind him his youngest wife, who was pregnant, but he took with him three other wives, several children and two mothers-in-law! His was no easy lot.

Clayton was quickly designated as general clerk of the "Camp of Israel," which meant that his record keeping would go on. He was frequently called upon to write letters, he had to create the reporting forms used by the clerks of the several pioneer companies, and he was responsible for instructing them in their duties. He also played a violin and presided over the band that often performed for the pioneers as well as for settlers on the Iowa plains. On top of all this and the countless tasks associated with caring for his family (his pregnant wife soon had her baby and joined the rest of the family), he kept a surprisingly detailed daily journal. At year's end he was camped at Winter Quarters, near the present Florence, Nebraska, and on April 14, 1847, he received the call from Brigham Young to join the vanguard company that would seek out the final spot for settlement in the Rocky Mountains. His multitude of jobs did not diminish as he traveled to the Salt Lake Valley and then, a few weeks after arriving there, returned to Winter Quarters slightly ahead of Brigham Young. On the outward journey he was appointed to assist Thomas Bullock, the official camp scribe, in keeping minutes. He was also assigned to write the journal of Heber C. Kimball, one of the Twelve Apostles of the Church. That alone was a time-consuming task, as he suggested in his own diary on May 21. He was already falling behind on the job, so Kimball told him to leave several pages blank for catching up and to start from that day to keep the diary current. "He furnished me a candle," the loyal scribe reported, "and I wrote the journal of this day's travel by candle light in his journal, leaving fifty-six pages blank." He also continued to keep his own personal journal, which was published by his family in 1921 and is one of the most complete and important accounts extant of this famous Mormon saga.

All this is offered in order to illustrate the persevering nature and reputation of William Clayton. He was not only a meticulous record keeper, with a well-deserved reputation as such among Church leaders, but he was also practically a slave to his work. He would not rest until he finished what he set about to do, and this no doubt accounted for much of the illness that plagued him not only on the pioneer journey but throughout his life. It was this quality that also resulted in the construction of the first roadometer among the Mormon pioneers and, finally, in the preparation of the *Emigrants' Guide*.

Brigham Young's pioneer company of 1847 was neither an exploring nor a trailblazing expedition. The route to the Great Basin was already well known, and at times the pioneers even saw signboards telling them how far they were from Fort Laramie. They also left their own signs for the benefit of following companies. They had with them a map of the West published by John C. Frémont, as well as Lansford Hastings' *Emigrants' Guide to Oregon and California*. The main difference between their path and the well-traveled Oregon Trail was that, until they got into Wyoming, they traveled on the north side of the Platte River while the Oregon pioneers were on the south. They simply wanted to avoid unnecessary contact with possibly unfriendly people.

As the vanguard company began moving westward, Clayton fretted over many details, but none bothered him quite so much as the lack of precision in recording the daily mileage. Were they not, after all, on God's errand, marking the path and determining the location of His people's refuge in the West? And were they not responsible for providing the best information possible to succeeding companies in order to facilitate the mass migration they were anticipating? How, then, in good conscience, could they even take a chance that their information would not be accurate? Estimates by different people varied as much as four miles a day, and Clayton was especially irritated when nearly everyone seemed to think that his estimates were too low. As early as April 19, four days after they started out, he suggested to Apostle Orson Pratt the idea of fastening a set of wooden cogs to a wagon wheel in order to measure the daily mileage accurately. Pratt seemed to like the thought, but nothing was done about it. Clayton was disgusted, but since he was not skilled enough in woodwork to construct the device he had suggested, he came up with his own very simple but tedious plan. On May 8 he measured one of the wheels on Heber Kimball's wagon, discovering to his amazement that 360 revolutions would constitute exactly one mile. He spent the whole day walking beside the wagon counting the revolutions of the wheel! The company had traveled eleven and a quarter miles, plus twenty revolutions, but, Clayton noted with a certain smug self-satisfaction, other people had estimated as much as thirteen or fourteen miles.

For the next three days he did the same thing, and also continued to nag his leaders until they took his suggestion for a mileage measuring machine seriously. Finally, on May 10, Brigham Young assigned Orson Pratt to give the subject some attention. Pratt, a mathematician, proposed what he called a "double-ended screw," which would attach to a wagon wheel and record up to thirty miles. Appleton Harmon, a skilled mechanic, was assigned to build it, which took two days. Clayton, meanwhile, continued the tiresome task of counting wagon wheel revolutions until, on May 12, the new device was installed. Then, two days later, came a petty and unfortunate argument. Harmon apparently began taking credit for the invention and Clayton quickly took offense. Actually, of course, credit belongs to all three men: Clayton, for suggesting the idea; Pratt, for devising the working plan; and Harmon, for his skill in constructing it and, in the process, making certain modifications that simplified its operation. A few months later, before Clayton began the return trip to Winter Quarters, the roadometer was further modified by William A. King so that it could record a thousand miles of travel.

The roadometer was absolutely essential for the completion of what came to be Clayton's most cherished pioneer project, *The Latter-day Saints' Emigrants' Guide.* We do not know when the idea first struck him, but it is interesting to observe how certain entries in his diary compare with the comments in the *Guide.* While enroute to the Salt Lake Valley he recorded grandiose, almost eloquent, descriptions of the countryside, but he also paid attention to details of the road as well as some camping spots. On June 10, for example, they camped at Deer Creek, which the *Guide* later said was exactly 619¾ miles from Winter Quarters. In his diary Clayton observed that it had plenty of timber on the banks, and an abundance of rich grass for the teams. He described the great fishing they found in the stream, as well as a rich bed of coal in the vicinity. The next day they crossed a "crooked, muddy creek," where they found "plenty of feed on the banks, but no wood.'"[1] In the *Guide* Deer Creek was described as a "lovely place to camp. Swift current, clear water, and abundance of fish. Nice grove of timber on the banks, and a coal mine about a quarter of a mile up, on the east side." A few miles further on it told its readers to look for "Crooked, muddy creek . . . Not good to cross — steep banks. Plenty of grass, but no wood." The diary accounts are not all that close to what is in the *Guide,* but it is clear that on the way to the valley Clayton was observing every detail of the road and what it meant for teams and wagons.

Before he left Salt Lake Valley to return to Winter Quarters Clayton was assigned officially to make a table of distances covering the entire route. He took the assignment seriously, even though some of his traveling companions seemingly took no interest in it at all. On the way out he had carefully watched and tended the roadometer. On the return trip he did it again, this time with an improved roadometer. Mileages in the *Guide* were based on the return trip's calculations, except for about twenty miles between Horse Creek and the La Bonte River. Ironically, the roadometer broke down both times he passed that stretch of the trail, so in that instance the *Guide* reflects his best estimate from the outgoing trip.

Obviously Clayton kept the mileage figures and other notes for his *Guide* separate from his diary, and because now he knew for sure that others would be using his work he made many more detailed observations on the way back to Winter Quarters. The *Guide* says, for example, that certain streams were dry on certain dates in the fall of 1847, and these happen to be the same dates that Clayton passed by on the return trip. Amid all the other things he had to do he carefully worked on the charts and text that would form the basis for his book. The day he arrived at Winter Quarters he observed that he was prepared "to make a complete traveler's guide from here to the Great Salt Lake, having been careful in taking the distance from creek to creek, over bluffs, mountains, etc." The entire distance was 1,032 miles.[2]

Clayton was not so altruistic that he could ignore the profit-making possibilities in the publication of such a guide — even if that profit came from selling it to his fellow Saints. His financial problems were serious, especially because he had a much larger than ordinary family to transport across the plains. He often brooded over his problems and, in spite of his faithful devotion to his Church leaders, sometimes convinced himself that he was being taken advantage of. On August 10 it all seemed to come to a head, as he indulged in one of the rare occasions where he poured out his negative feelings in his diary. That day Heber Kimball gave him a pair of trousers as a present, but deep in his troubled soul Clayton wondered whether the balance sheet was really even. He had the somewhat paranoid impression that Kimball and others believed he had already been repaid for all his work, for others had provided his transportation, shelter and food along the way, and that he was along only for the good times the trip provided. He could no longer resist expressing his resentment:

> Now how much have I done for Brother Kimball? Am I justly indebted on this journey? Answer: I have written in his journal 124 pages of close matter on an average of 600 words to a page, which if paid at the price of recording deeds in Illinois would amount to over $110.00. I have collected the matter myself, besides writing letters, etc. This has been for his special benefit. I have kept an account of the distance we have traveled for over 800 miles of the journey, attended to the measurement of the road, kept the distances from creek to creek and from one encampment to another; put up a guide board every ten miles from Fort John [Laramie] to this place with the assistance of Philo Johnson. I have mapped some for Dr. Richards and keeping my own journal forms the whole benefit to be derived by my family by this mission. I have yet considerable to write in Elder Kimball's journal before I return. I am expected to keep a table of distances of the whole route returning from here to Winter Quarters and make a map when I get through, and this for public benefit. Now how much am I considered to be in debt, and how often will it be said that I was furnished by others with victuals, clothing, etc., that I might enjoy this journey as a mission of pleasure.[3]

Clayton arrived at Winter Quarters on October 21. Almost immediately the Mormons there recognized the value of his manuscript,

and began to ask for copies. He declined, however, for he wanted
Brigham Young's approval before he distributed it at all. Besides,
finally he could see a profit-making potential in his work, and the
two days it took to make one copy would "put it out of the reach of
profit if I was inclined to help myself a little by it."[4] He nevertheless made one copy for Brigham Young, sent it to the Church leader
with an invitation to suggest improvements, and asked permission
to sell a few copies.

Even though he heard nothing from Brigham Young for over two
months, Clayton went ahead with plans to publish the work. By
early February he was ready to take it to St. Louis and find a publisher, though he still wanted his Church leader's approval as well
as a letter of introduction. He finally got both. The letter was ad-
dressed to Nathaniel H. Felt, presiding elder over the Church in
St. Louis, and a certain Mr. William Pickert (or Picket). It intro-
duced Clayton and his project, verified the desire of Church leaders
to have the guide published, and asked the recipients to help in any
way possible. "By getting the same published it will be but a very
trifling expence to the Emigrating Saints in comparison to the labor
of handscribing same for each company."[5] The importance of Clayton's work was obvious, for it would prove invaluable to every pioneer company that hoped to join the Mormons in their Rocky
Mountain refuge.

On February 10 William Clayton was on his way to St. Louis,
along with Lucius N. Scovil. Nineteen days later they arrived, and in
a short time Clayton was able to arrange with the publishing house
of Chambers & Knapp to print 5,000 copies of the *Guide*. They sold
quickly, as not only Clayton himself but also others, such as his good
friend Thomas Bullock, peddled them among the Saints in the
spring of 1848. A year later a Utah settler wrote a friend in Missouri
what must have been a typical reaction:

> If you could have learned the great demand there has
> been for the Guide . . . and could have had them on the
> road, they would have brought a good piece. Five dollars
> is what they have been sold for, but twenty-five dollars
> has been offered for them, and they could not be had. The
> emigrants say that they have realized great advantages
> from them, and if they had to travel this route again, they
> would gladly give twenty-five dollars, rather than be with-
> out them. I have only got a few here, and I shall not take
> for them less than $2.00 a piece. I wish I had some more,

and when you, or any of you come, I wish you to bring
four or five hundred of them.[6]

The letter writer was not exaggerating, for the little book was indeed a marvelously detailed and helpful guide to every mile the emigrant would travel. Every major stream, hill, swamp, or other landmark was listed, and brief descriptions were given of what might be
found there. Suggestions were given as to campsites, watering
places and forage, and Clayton was very careful to tell his readers
how and where to cross the streams. In addition, he told them how
far away they were from Winter Quarters, how far to the next landmark, and the distance from each landmark to the City of the Great
Salt Lake. He also included longitude, latitude and altitude for many
locations. Who could ask for more?

We are not aware of how many editions were printed for pioneer
use, but Clayton reported in 1852 that a new edition had just been
issued and was selling for fifty cents. Apparently, however, this was
an unauthorized printing for, he complained, he had offered to sell
the copyright to the press of Fisher and Bennett "but they considered themselves perfectly safe without it." At the time, Clayton
was on his way to England as a missionary and intended to sell the
work there. After all, most of the European Mormons emigrating to
America must pass through Liverpool, and Clayton expected to
beat Fisher and Bennett to the market and "spoil their speculations."[7] His unexpected quick return from England, however,
spoiled his own speculations.

It was not only the Mormons who profited from Clayton's guide.
When Joseph E. Ware published *The Emigrant's Guide to California* in 1849 he abridged with hardly any change in wording Clayton's description of the five hundred miles between Fort Laramie
and the Bear River. "Plagiarism," commented western historian
John Caughey when he later edited Ware's work, "but from the
best handbook for this section of the trail."[8] Thousands of pioneers
bound for Oregon also used Clayton's guide for portions of their
journey. The original edition has practically disappeared, "presum-
ably," commented one editor, "from the fact that the copies were
read to pieces." Its significance has not been lost, however, and
several facsimile printings have been made, even as late as 1974.[9]

Clayton lived the rest of his life in Salt Lake City, where he made
his livelihood in a number of public and private capacities. He was
territorial auditor and territorial recorder of marks and brands. He

served as treasurer for the Deseret Telegraph Company and secretary of the Church-owned Zion's Cooperative Mercantile Institution. He also engaged in such private business activities as debt collection, money lending, merchandising, lumbering, farming and mining. He died in 1879 at the age of 65.

The meticulous care and sense of duty with which Clayton always worked resulted in an important contribution to the saga of the West, and The Patrice Press is to be applauded for recognizing this and providing the present fine edition of his *Guide*. This is the only edition to have been published with careful editorial comments such as those provided by Professor Stanley B. Kimball. Hopefully, the combined skills of Clayton and Kimball will help the modern reader come closer than ever before to feeling the concerns, the excitement and the drama of the Mormon pioneers as they followed step-by-step in the path of that vanguard company of 1847.

FOOTNOTES

[1] William Clayton, *William Clayton's Journal* (Salt Lake City: The Clayton Family Association, 1921), 229-31.

[2] Ibid., 376

[3] Ibid., 343-4

[4] William Clayton to Brigham Young, 15 November 1847, LDS Church Archives, Salt Lake City, Utah.

[5] A copy of this letter is in the William Clayton papers, Church Archives. It is apparently an original draft, for it contains numerous line outs and corrections.

[6] *The Missouri Republican,* St. Louis, 3 October 1849.

[7] William Clayton, "Missionary Journal, 1852-53," entry of 26 November 1852, Church Archives.

[8] Joseph E. Ware, *The Emigrants' Guide to California,* reprinted from the 1849 edition with Introduction and Notes by John Caughey (Princeton: Princeton University Press, 1932), 20n.

[9] In 1974 a beautiful facsimile edition of the *Emigrants' Guide* was published by Ye Galleon Press, Fairfield, Washington. Only three hundred copies were printed. The quotation above is on page 26. The publisher noted that only about ten copies of the original edition still exist.

THE PIONEER ODOMETER.

This machine was invented by two of the Pioneers who crossed the Great Plains in 1847, and was used by Brigham Young and his company to measure the distance from the Missouri River to Salt Lake Valley. The difference between the measurements made with this instrument and those made by the government surveyors, who subsequently passed over the route, was less than 60 feet.

THE PIONEER ODOMETER: This odometer is probably the second one made, the one which Clayton used to measure the distances on the return trip from the Valley of the Great Salt Lake. The original odometer used going west has apparently disappeared. This machine is on exhibit in the Museum of Church History and Art, Salt Lake City, Utah.

THE
LATTER-DAY SAINTS'
EMIGRANTS' GUIDE

THE EDITOR'S PREFACE

A S OUR NATIONAL HERITAGE DISAPPEARS there seems to be a direct relationship between the rapidity with which we destroy this legacy and our desire to write and read about it, even to go in search of it. Nowhere is this more true than with our great western trails. For over twenty years interest has been growing in them, excellent books have been published, preservation and historical societies have been organized, and there is no evidence that this special and general interest is waning. In 1968, for example, Congress enacted the National Trails System Act (Public Law 90-543) and The Patrice Press is one of several publishers devoted almost exclusively to trail publications.

Clayton's guide to the Mormon Trail (as distinct from the Oregon Trail) has seldom been appreciated for what it was and is. It needs to be better known and put into proper perspective. His twenty-four-page, pocket-size paperback booklet of 1848 was simply the first practical and best emigrant guide of its day to the great Far West. (Clayton also kept a journal along with his guide and it, too, has become famous — see pp. 32-33. Furthermore, in 1846, while the Pioneers were crossing Iowa, he wrote the words to the most renowned of all Mormon hymns, "Come, Come, Ye Saints," often called the "Mormon Marseillaise." The verses epitomize the Mormon motivation for going west. The words and music for this hymn are reproduced on page 101.)

Although possessed of no special qualifications for such a work, Clayton came to his task rather naturally. An English convert to Mormonism in 1837, he immigrated to Nauvoo, Illinois in 1840 where he served in many capacities as a clerk, eventually assisting the Mormon Prophet, Joseph Smith.

In 1846, when Brigham Young led the Mormons west from

Illinois, Clayton was appointed "Clerk of the Camp of Israel" and kept a very sketchy journal of the trek across Iowa, that Mormon Mesopotamia between the Mississippi and Missouri rivers.

The following April 15, when the Mormon Pioneers of 1847 pushed on to the Far West on their 111-day, 1,032-mile trek from Civilization to Sundown in search of their new Zion, Clayton became one of the historians of that company of 143 men, 3 women and 2 children. Perhaps at Brigham Young's insistence, Clayton's journal of this portion of The Exodus was five times as long as his Iowa account.[1]

Part of Clayton's responsibility was to keep an accurate record of distances traveled daily, campsites, and any other information which would be helpful to the thousands of other Mormons Young expected would follow him west. Although there is no evidence that any formal published guide was thought of at this time, it is clear that Clayton's journal was planned as a source of useful information for future westering Mormons.

It is this concern over subsequent emigrants which helps make the Mormon emigrant movement unique. Not only did Mormons not go west for furs, gold, land, adventure, or a new identity, they did not even want to go. Furthermore, the Pioneers of 1847 were not concerned with just a one-way passage for themselves as were most who went west. They were charting and improving a road for thousands of converts who followed for over twenty years, until the coming of the railroad in 1869.

At first Clayton merely guessed the distance traveled daily, a most unsatisfactory practice which led to many disputes. But on May 8 he measured a wagon wheel which was 14 feet 8 inches in circumference, or, fortuitously, exactly 1/360th of a mile. To this he tied a piece of red flannel and began the mind-stultifying, but accurate, business of counting the revolutions. A few days later an idea Clayton had been toying with since at least April 19 began to take shape. This consisted of a system of cogs mounted on a wagon wheel for measuring distance. By May 13 and 14 this contraption, called an "odometer" or "roadometer," was installed and worked rather imperfectly, on and off, until the Pioneers reached the Valley of the Great Salt Lake.

Probably as a result of his conception of an odometer Clayton was asked on May 18 to make a map of the Pioneer route. Lacking cartographic skills and not knowing how to coordinate his measurements with the Frémont-Preuss maps the Pioneers had with them and the astronomical observations made by a member of the Mormon company, Clayton suggested that he wait until the return journey and try to make a new map not based on Frémont's. By July 3, Clayton had "made out a table of distance between creeks and camp grounds,"[2] which may have been the genesis of his later *Guide.*

Orson Pratt, a Mormon with some astronomical and engineering skills, served informally as the Pioneers' "scientific member," and had been making sightings along the Mormon Trail from Nauvoo. His latitudinal determinations, according to his journal, were made alternately by "meridian observation of Sirius," by "altitude of the Pole Star," by "meridian observation of the sun," and by "the meridian altitude of the moon." They are generally quite accurate, for west of the Missouri at least he had excellent instruments especially ordered from England. Lacking a suitable chronometer, however, his few longitudinal sightings made by the "angular distance of the sun and moon taken by sextant and circle" cannot be trusted. Even Fremont, who often spent hours making multiple sightings of the occultations of the planets and stars by the moon and of the Jupiterian satellites, had difficulty determining proper longitude. He had to later redo much of his early work. Along the Platte River a miscalculation of only one minute causes an error of 6,000 feet in latitude and 4,500 feet in longitude.

After reaching the Valley of the Great Salt Lake it was necessary to make another roadometer and test it out. This second one appears to have worked much better and on August 10 Clayton recorded in his journal, "I am expected to keep a table of distances of the whole route returning from here to Winter Quarters and make a map when I get through, and this for public benefit." (See illustration, p. 10.)

One week later Clayton left the valley with a slow moving ox team company of 71 men and 33 wagons. This was ten days before Young started on the return journey; the two parties never traveled together. This means that not only were Clayton's calculations made returning east, a route differing in parts from the Pioneer route going west, but they were not necessarily identical with the route Young took on his return.

By October 31 all of the Pioneers who had not remained in the valley were back in Winter Quarters and the winter was spent in staying alive and preparing for a spring removal of the Mormons still in the Winter Quarters area. So many of these Mormons wanted copies of Clayton's notes on the route that he recorded in the preface to his *Guide,* "The labor of writing a copy being considerable, as well as requiring much time — it was concluded to publish it in its present form, by which means it can be afforded at a price which will bring it within reach of any person wishing to have it.''

Such then is the background of the manuscript and the motivation for Clayton leaving Winter Quarters early in 1848 (on Feb. 10, as Professor Allen has discovered) by riverboat to go to St. Louis to have 5,000 copies of his guide published. (There is no evidence he ever prepared a map to accompany the guide.)

Specific information about Clayton's stay in St. Louis has failed to turn up. His preface is dated "St. Louis, Mo., 13th March, 1848,'' which is probably the day he turned the manuscript over to the printer, or perhaps the date he secured the copyright. Three St. Louis daily newspapers, the *Missouri Republican,* the *St. Louis Daily Union,* and the *St. Louis Daily New Era* do not list him in their daily "hotel guests" column, and carry no ads or any notice at all of his publication. (Since he chose as his printer Chambers and Knapp at 11 Chestnut St., between Main and Second streets, who also owned and printed the *Missouri Republican,* one would think some notice might have appeared in that paper.)[3]

Obviously Clayton stayed with some of the hundreds of Mormons then in St. Louis (to whom he had a letter of introduction) who were preparing to go west in 1848. He returned to Winter Quarters with his publications, not bothering to try and sell them in St. Louis.

There is even a question as to how Clayton marketed his guide among Mormons. In the United States there was no official Mormon newspaper from February 15, 1846, when the Mormons were quitting Nauvoo, and February 7, 1849, when the *Frontier Guardian* commenced in Kanesville (now Council Bluffs), Iowa. Although this paper advertised many goods and services appropriate to Mormon and non-Mormon emigrants, no reference to Clayton's *Guide* was found in it. In over 700 Mormon trail accounts I also found no reference regarding the distribution of this guide.

Equally surprising is the fact that no significant reference to it was found in the *Millennial Star,* an official Mormon bimonthly published in England. The editor, Orson Pratt, was a member of the original Pioneer company of 1847 and published his own Pioneer journal in 1849 and 1850 in the *Star.* Furthermore, Pratt could not have been ignorant of the fact that thousands from Great Britain would follow in the tracks of the Pioneers and would need such a book.[4] Nor did I find any reference to this *Guide* in the *Deseret News,* an official Mormon newspaper which commenced publication in Salt Lake City June 15, 1850. Most likely it was handled by Mormon emigration agents and, as Allen has noted, by Clayton himself and his friends.

One would assume that Clayton's work was popular with Mormons, yet in my study of Mormon trail accounts I found but three incidental references to his *Guide*. Of course many foreign emigrants could not have read the booklet had they had it and after a few years the trail was so well known that many emigrants felt such guides to be unnecessary. Furthermore, most Mormon companies were accompanied by trail-wise Saints who, perhaps, needed no guides.

There is some evidence that many non-Mormons, especially California gold seekers, used this guide. George Washington Averett, one of the few Mormons to join the Gold Rush of 1849, for example, wrote in his journal, "Our company having for their guide what we called the Mormon Guide found to be most reliable of any we could find, having several others in our company, Frémont and Bryant's neither of them being so reliable as the Mormon Guide." Averett is referring to the famous *Reports* of John C. Frémont and to Edwin Bryant's *What I Saw In California . . . in the Years, 1846-1847:* New York, 1848. The later work is a 455-page travel account, *sans* maps or tables, hardly a practical guide.

Not surprisingly Clayton had a very high opinion of his work. In his preface he noted, "Many works have been published, and maps exhibited for the instruction of emigrants, but none which ever pretended to set forth the particulars contained in this work, so far as regards the route from Council Bluffs to the Great Salt Lake."

Let us now attempt to assess the truth of Clayton's opinion, to evaluate the "Many works . . . and maps" to which he refers, to discern from what sources he drew, to discover with what contemporary frontiersmen he may have consulted, to briefly trace the genesis and development of the Mormon plan to go west, and to note what influence Clayton's *Guide* had on other writers — in short, to place Clayton's work in its proper perspective.

The usual place to start the story of the Mormons and the Rocky Mountains is with a statement of August 6, 1842, which Joseph Smith allegedly made: "I prophesied that the Saints would continue to suffer much affliction and would be driven to the Rocky Mountains. . . ." There are claims that he said something similar as early as 1838 or even 1834. Many, in fact, have taken comfort in, and indeed still take comfort in the idea that the move to the West was in fulfillment of some prophecy. These early allegations, however, need not concern us here.[5] We are on firmer ground and dealing with more germane material if we start no earlier than July 1843, when Smith sent Jonathan Dunbar to investigate a route across Iowa from Nauvoo, Illinois to the Missouri River. By February 1844 Smith had also suggested an exploring party be sent to investigate locations for possible settlement to California and Oregon. In March 1844, he sent a memorial to Congress requesting authorization to raise 100,000 armed volunteers "for the protection of citizens [Mormons] in the United States emigrating to the territories [Texas and Oregon]."

For several reasons nothing came of the projected exploring party or the memorial. Among other things, Smith began campaigning for the presidency of the United States, Congress refused to receive the memorial, and Joseph was murdered the following June by an anti-Mormon mob.

One important event, however, did come from the abortive memorial. Congressman Stephen A. Douglas from Illinois did give to Joseph's petitioner, Orson Hyde, and also sent to Joseph, a "map of Oregon, and also a report on the exploration of the country lying between the Missouri River and the Rocky Mountains . . . by Lieut. John C. Frémont." (A copy of this map appears on pp. 96-97.) Such was the beginning of the Mormon acquaintance with Frémont's *Reports* and maps. (It is not known whether Smith ever saw Frémont's *Report,* for he was killed about a month after Hyde's letter was received.)[6]

The death of Joseph ended further discussion of going West for the rest of that year and the church as a whole dedicated itself to effecting the plans of its martyred prophet — completing the temple, building a better Nauvoo, and expanding the proselytizing program.

By January 1845, however, it appears that Brigham Young, Joseph's *de facto* if not *de jure* successor and other Mormon leaders carried on simultaneously two mutually exclusive programs: (1) to build up Nauvoo, and (2) to prepare to leave. Until October 1845, however, the second program was not generally known. That Young was preparing his followers for such a move is manifested by the fact that on October 30, 1844, the *Nauvoo Neighbor,* a Mormon newspaper, printed a selection from Washington Irving's *Astoria* entitled "The Climate of the Rocky Mountains," and that throughout 1845 the same paper published many other articles on Oregon, the Indians, and especially extracts from Frémont's *Reports* about the Oregon Trail, the Bear River area, and the Valley of the Great Salt Lake. Also published were portions of Lansford W. Hastings' *Emigrants' Guide to Oregon and California,* which had just appeared in 1845. Furthermore the *New York Messenger,* another Mormon publication, printed between July and September 1845, in a nine-part series, almost the entirety of Hastings' book.[7] Young even revived Smith's proposal about sending out a party to search for locations in the West, but nothing came of it.

How long Young intended to carry on both programs is not known, for his hand was forced that fall. During September 1845 anti-Mormons, convinced that the Mormons were not going to leave Illinois, commenced a program of harassment. More than 200 Mormon homes and farm buildings located outside Nauvoo were burned that fall and the anti-Mormon convention headquartered in Carthage decreed that the Mormons must quit Illinois the following spring. Therefore, on October 4 a western exploring party was organized and during a general conference of the church held that month the exodus was officially announced and scheduled for the spring of 1846.

Mormon historical records show that on December 20, 1845, Apostle Franklin D. Richards "read Frémont's Journal giving an account of his travels to California," to Young and "a few of the Twelve [apostles]," that on December 27 "Elder Parley P. Pratt read from Hastings' account of California," and that on December 29 "Elder Parley P. Pratt read Frémont's *Journal* to Brother [Heber C.] Kimball and me [Young]." A notation for New Year's Eve deserves to be cited in full: "Elder Heber C. Kimball and I [Young] superintended the operation in the Temple, examined *maps,* with reference to selecting a location for the saints west of the Rocky Mountains, and reading *various works,* written by travelers in those regions."[8] (Italics added.) For a discussion of these maps and works see pp. 20-27.

Even after quitting Nauvoo during February 1846, the advance group of Mormons continued to gather information about the West. That July, shortly after the Pioneers had reached the Missouri River, Col. T.L. Kane, a young Philadelphian friend and self-appointed guardian of the Saints, was in their midst and later sent them presents and "Capt. Frémont's topographical map of the road to Oregon for the use of the pioneers."[9] There is also evidence that David Atchison, who had befriended the Mormons in 1838 in Missouri and who was then a senator from Missouri, also sent Young a copy of Frémont's 1845 map.[10]

Furthermore, on January 6, 1847, Young wrote to a Church member in St. Louis: "I want you to bring me one half dozen of Mitchell's new map of Texas, Oregon & California and the regions adjoining, or his accompaniment for the same for 1846, or rather the latest edition and best map of all the Indian countries in North America . . . If there is anything later or better than Mitchell's, I want the best.''[11] (For a discussion of this map and also of the frontiersmen the Mormons consulted with see pp. 27, 28-29.)

This brief sketch regarding the Mormons' plans and preparations for going west raises some fascinating questions about which maps and works they were familiar with and consulted. Obviously they were acquainted with Irving's *Astoria,* Frémont's *Reports* and maps, and with Hastings' book. Professors James Allen and Glen Leonard have noted that along with Fremont's, ''three other maps hung on the walls of the temple'' in Nauvoo and that church leaders ''were also familiar with the expeditions of Charles Wilkes and B.L.E. Bonneville.''[12]

In order to better understand just what maps and works were consulted we must examine the trans-Missouri travel/guide literature available to Mormon leaders generally through April 1847, when they left the Missouri River for the Far West. We are also concerned with the material available to William Clayton through the time of publication of his *Guide* — February 1848.

Probably the Mormons were not even aware of much of the literature, still less able to consult it, but it will be helpful nonetheless to survey the field.

Travel literature had had a long and honorable vogue in the young republic. Dozens of guides appeared between a 1748 guide to Kentucky and throughout the nineteenth century to one to the Klondike goldfields in 1897. However, the Mormons probably consulted nothing prior to the appearance in 1814 of Meriwether Lewis' *The Lewis and Clark Expedition.* Although the Mormons in general would have learned little of value from this publication, Clayton might very well have been influenced by Meriwether Lewis' eight-page ''Summary Statement of Rivers, Creeks and most Remarkable places, their distance from each other, etc..'' This was a five-column table giving ''Names of remarkable places, Widths of rivers and creeks, Sides on which they were situated, Distance from one another, and Distance from the Mississippi.'' Perhaps Clayton got his idea for arranging his guide in such a columnar form from Lewis.

Had the Mormons read H.M. Brackenridge's 1816 *Journal of A Voyage up the River Missouri* . . . they would have gleaned about three pages of very general references to the Platte River and a quaint story that Missouri rivermen indulged in horseplay with first timers passing the mouth of the Platte River, much as ocean voyagers did when crossing the equator for the first time. Clayton, however, might have been interested in Brackenridge's "A Table of Distances," which was almost identical in form to Lewis' except that it added one important additional column for "Latitude."

In 1819 John Bradbury published his *Travels in the Interior of America* . . . which would have given the Mormons some very general information about the mouth of the Platte River.

Perhaps the earliest publication of specific value to the Mormons would have been Edwin James' 1823 *Account of an Expedition from Pittsburgh to the Rocky Mountains,* based on the notes of Maj. S.H. Long of the famous U.S. Army Corps of Topographical Engineers. This work detailed Long's 1820 expedition from a point on the Missouri about ten miles above the later site of the Mormon Winter Quarters, westward along a line of march very similar to that of the Mormons in 1847; that is, along the *north* bank of the Platte — across the Elkhorn River and Shell Creek, past the Pawnee Villages, the ford of the Loup River, and continuing west along the north bank of the Platte to the confluence of the North and South Platte branches. That is where Long turned southwest into present-day Colorado (and discovered Long's Peak.) The forty-two-page account of this part of Long's expedition and his map would surely have been one of the best works the Mormons could have consulted, for this was the best exploring account of the Great Plains before Frémont.

In 1831 Hall J. Kelly published a *General Circular* and *A Geographical Sketch* regarding Oregon which would have been of no use whatsoever to the Mormons save for his recommendation that the mouth of the Platte River was a good point of departure.

In 1836 the *Journal* and map of Col. Henry Dodge's expedition along the Oregon Trail from Fort Leavenworth to the forks of the Platte (and into present-day Colorado) was published. Except for information about the Pawnees, the Mormons would have learned little from this publication.

One year later, in 1837, the imagination of the nation was caught by Washington Irving's reworking of the 1833 journal of Capt. Benjamin Louis Eulalie de Bonneville into *The Adventures of Captain Bonneville in the Rocky Mountains and the Far West.* The account of the Oregon Trail between Fort Laramie and the Green River would have been of some value to the Mormons. Of special interest would have been the five-page description of the Great Salt Lake provided for Bonneville by one of his men, Joseph W.R. Walker. Despite the fact that his name was attached to the ancient Lake Bonneville, the captain never saw the Salt Lake. However, Bonneville was the first to prove the feasibility of taking loaded wagons over the famed South Pass. As has already been noted, we have reason to believe that the Mormon leaders were acquainted with this publication.

The following year a book appeared which the Mormons might have known of. This was the Rev. Samuel Parker's *Journal of an Exploring Tour Beyond the Rocky Mountains* along the Oregon Trail from Fort Leavenworth to the Green River via Bellevue; that is, across the Papillion, Elkhorn, the Loup, and along the *north* side of the Platte to Fort Laramie — the same way the Mormons later went. The reverend gentleman's thirty-one-page account from Bellevue to the Green River would have been most helpful to the Mormons had they seen it.

In 1839 there appeared John K. Townsend's *Narrative of a Journey Across the Rocky Mountains* . . . along the Oregon Trail to the Bear River. The ten-page account of his route between the future site of Fort Laramie and the Green River would have been of marginal use to the Mormons, for Townsend had in mind readers, not emigrants. The 1843 appearance of *Travels in the Interior of North America,* by Maximilian, Prince of Wied, would have meant nothing to the Mormons, and the Mormons would have gleaned little from George Wilkes' 1843 *The History of Oregon* other than his two-page "Resolutions," a sort of traveling compact. They would not have learned much from Father Pierre Jean De Smet's 1843 *Letters and Sketches . . . of the Rocky Mountains* or from his *Oregon Missions and Travels over the Rocky Mountains* of 1847. (As will be noted on page 28, however, the Mormons learned from a personal visit with De Smet.)

Had the Saints been fortunate enough to have read the *New York Spirit of the Times* from November 1844 through April 1845, they would have learned much from the pen of Lt. J. Henry Carleton of a company of dragoons which spent some time in 1844 with the Pawnees along the Loup River. They would also have gathered a good description of the Indian trail from Bellevue to the Loup River, which they would travel in 1847. However, it is very unlikely they ever heard of the young officer of the dragoons.[13]

Thomas J. Farnham's 1843 publication of his trip to Oregon via Colorado, *Travels in the . . . Rocky Mountains,* would have helped the Mormons not at all, for he also had readers, not emigrants, in mind. Of far more importance was another publication in 1843, the first part of a work which was probably worth as much to the Mormons as everything else published to that date combined. I refer, of course, to Capt. John C. Frémont's *A Report of the Exploring Expeditions to the Rocky Mountains in the Year 1842.* This was the Frémont *Report* mentioned so often by the Mormons. A 10,000-copy edition was reprinted in 1845 as the first part of his *A Report of the Exploring Expedition to the Rocky Mountains in the Year 1842 and To Oregon and North California in the Years 1843-44.* The seventy-nine-page *Report* of 1843 was the first scientific survey of the Oregon Trail and the first reasonably accurate guidebook to the West. Of special value to the Mormons was the accompanying Frémont-Preuss map (see pp. 96-97).

The 1843 *Report* was useful to the Mormons for its account of the Platte River Valley from present-day North Platte, Nebraska, to South Pass. Of most value to the Mormons in the subsequent 1845 *Report* was not the three-page account of the route from South Pass to the Bear River, but his account of the exploration of the Great Salt Lake (which he reached via the soda springs), the Bear River area, and the Valley of the Great Salt Lake. Of paramount interest to the Mormons were his comments on the fertility of the valleys west of the Rocky Mountains. Frémont's short, four-column "Table of Distances" might have suggested to Clayton the form his guide would take.

Next to Frémont the most often mentioned source of information to the Mormons was Lansford W. Hastings' *The Emigrant's Guide to Oregon and California,* also published in 1845. For all of the fame or notoriety of this work, it is difficult to see wherein its value to the Mormons lay. His short account of his traveling from St. Louis to the Green River would have been of small help to the Mormons. He devoted exactly one sentence on pp. 137-138 to what became the famous and infamous Hastings Cutoff, "The most direct route for the California Emigrants, would be to leave the Oregon route, about two hundred miles east from Fort Hall; then bearing west-south-west, to the Salt Lake; and thence continuing down to the bay of San Francisco, by the route just described." Nevertheless, this one sentence sent some to their deaths and suggested to the Mormons a shorter way to the Valley of the Great Salt Lake west from Fort Bridger, rather than via Fort Hall. The Mormons might also have found very valuable Hastings' excellent ten-page chapter on "The Equipment, Supplies, and the Method of Traveling."

Since Hastings has become the regulation villain among those who, for whatever reasons, encouraged Americans to go west, and since his 1845 work was so well known by the westerning Mormons, let us examine briefly just what he did do. A writer and a lawyer from Ohio, in 1842 he helped lead what some call "the first planned overland wagon migration to Oregon." From Oregon he went to California in 1843. There he became so enthusiastic about the potential of the area and his possible future there that he wrote his book and went east in 1845 via Mexico, to have it published. He returned to California that same year. There he met Frémont, who had just blazed a trail from the Great Salt Lake to Pilot Peak in Nevada (a trail which would become a part of Hastings' proposed cutoff). Hastings was so much encouraged by talking with Frémont over the feasibility of his proposed cutoff that he returned east in 1846, this time to actually check out his "direct route." Eastward from the Great Salt Lake he proceeded, to use modern toponyms, up Parley's Canyon, over Big Mountain, down Little Emigration Canyon, up East and Main canyons to Henefer on the Weber River, up Echo Canyon, crossing the Bear River near Evanston, and then to Fort Bridger. There he convinced at least five emigrating parties to try his cutoff. Hastings advised or guided all five parties. Four of them made it successfully to California, passing through the Rocky Mountains via the Weber River with great difficulty.

The fifth did not follow the Weber route because Hastings personally showed one of their party the way west from the Weber. This was the Reed-Donner party, forty-four of whom perished in Sierra snows. Their deaths have been blamed largely on Hastings, and this is somewhat unfair. Their late start, lack of both organization and cooperation among themselves also contributed to their fate. Perhaps Hastings' culpability should be limited to the fact he tragically failed to realize that oxen hauling heavy wagons across a desert is far different from men crossing on horseback.

Two other studies appeared in 1845, neither of which could have been of much help to the Mormons. One was the eleven-page *Report* of Col. S.W. Kearny's summer campaign to the Rocky Mountains; the other was a five-volume *Narrative of the U.S. Exploring Expedition* . . . by Capt. Charles Wilkes of the United States Navy, who commanded six ships and a corps of scientists and naturalists. They spent three years in the South Pacific and the Antarctic before proceeding to the Oregon area. As already noted, the Mormons in Nauvoo were familiar with this study. (Perhaps Douglas had sent them a copy.) They would have been interested in Wilkes' study of Oregon in volume four.

While the Mormons were crossing Iowa and setting up Winter Quarters in 1846 three additional works appeared which somehow might have been secured from St. Louis. The best was *Route Across the Rocky Mountains* by Overton Johnson and William H. Winter. For 176 pages they appear to have had the armchair traveler in mind, but a two-part appendix reveals their concern for the practical. Following eight pages of "Instructions to Emigrants — Supplies and Equipment — Manner of Traveling, &c," is a ten-page "Bill of Route" which would have been an excellent model for Clayton. In four columns it lists places or topographic features, distances between them, a cumulative trail of miles traveled, brief descriptions of each site, and what might be called "notes" on the road, wood, grass, water, landmarks and similar necessary observations — the same type of information Clayton later provided. (See page 100 for a sample page from that work.)

J.M. Shivley's very short nine-page *Route and Distances to Oregon and California* was a serious attempt to produce a real guide, not a book for armchair travelers, and is about as good as could be expected from something that brief. His first three and one-half pages provide helpful hints on how to prepare for the serious business of westering; the balance presents a brief description of the Oregon road, topographic features, and campsites. It concluded with a one-page table of "Distances from Independence to Astoria." Perhaps Clayton was also inspired by this little work.

Rufus B. Sage's highly literate *Scenes in the Rocky Mountains* offered vivid word pictures, good reading, and little else to the Mormons which they could not have found elsewhere.

The Pioneers of 1847 could not have benefitted from Joel Palmer's excellent account of the Oregon Trail, *Journal of Travels over the Rocky Mountains . . .* published that same year. Clayton, however, might very well have later after returning from the West. He may have become familiar with its "Table of Distances from Independence, Missouri; and St. Joseph, to Oregon City, in Oregon Territory," which also included brief notations regarding campsites, the road, fuel and water.

A survey of the maps available to the Pioneers and to Clayton will help determine what several maps might have been hanging on the walls of the temple and what maps might have been taken west by the Pioneers. There were many available — a plethora in fact. Since at least 1722 dozens of Spanish, French and American maps had been published showing, in varying degrees of accuracy and fullness, the Platte River area. Over fifty maps of the trans-Mississippi West appeared during the first five years of the 1840s, and in the critical year of 1846 another twenty-eight were published.

From a practical standpoint there is no use in this study to consider anything published prior to the 1814 Lewis and Clark map, which sketched out the Platte Valley. So did Roberdeau's "sketch" of 1818, Bradbury's map and Tanner's of 1822. Probably the first map the Mormons would have taken seriously was Maj. S.H. Long's of 1823, which not only gave details along the north side of the Platte from the Missouri River to the forks of the Platte, but is also generally considered to have been his best map of the Platte area prior to the Frémont-Preuss work. (A copy of this map appears on page 94-95.)

Of the maps published during the 1830s it appears the Mormons did consult the 1835 map of Bonneville. Unfortunately he was an untrained amateur and his map, not based on astronomical observations, is of poor technical quality; still it was widely known and used in its day. Gallatin, who never left New York City, produced a vague and amateurish map in 1836. Two maps appeared in 1838; one by M.H. Stansbury was of limited value, but one by Samuel Parker clearly showed the connections between the Loup, Platte, Sweetwater, Sandy, Green, and Bear Rivers.

While there were many maps of the trans-Missouri West published in the 1840s, almost every one the Mormons might have been interested in were either those of Frémont-Preuss or those based on Frémont-Preuss. The three Frémont-Pruess maps which appeared in 1843, 1845, and 1846, were what we would call strip maps today, showing only the area actually explored with no attempt to present wide, general areas. They represent the best American cartography between Long's work and the Civil War.

The first of the Frémont-Preuss series, showing the Oregon Trail in great detail from the forks of the Platte to South Pass and the Wind River Mountains, was the basis for the two which followed. In large format, 14½" by 33¾", it was clearly the finest map of that area ever produced. Preuss prepared another map in 1845 to accompany Frémont's second *Report* of that year. As the 1845 publication included the 1843 material, the 1845 map embodied everything on the 1843 map. In huge format, 51" x 31½", it showed his route along the Oregon Trail from Westport (now part of Kansas City), to South Pass, Fort Vancouver, and on to San Francisco Bay. This map also provided a good sketch of the Platte River west from Bellevue, showing the Elkhorn, Loup, and Wood rivers.

In 1846 Preuss reworked his 1845 map and produced another map compiled "from the field notes of Cpt. J.C. Frémont and from sketches and notes made on the ground by his assistant Charles Preuss," which was issued as a public document by order of the U.S. Senate.

This map, from Westport to the Columbia River, was constructed on a grand scale of only ten miles to the inch and issued in seven sections, each 26″ by 16″. There is good reason to conclude that the Pioneers successively acquired all three maps and had them with them during The Exodus.

Of those maps derived from Frémont-Preuss which the Mormons may have also consulted are products which appeared with the 1845 *Report* of Col. S.W. Kearny's expedition from Fort Leavenworth to South Pass; the 1845 Charles Wilkes Map of Oregon Territory; Rufus B. Sage's 1846 Map of Oregon, California, New Mexico and Northwest Texas; and above all, one or more of the three maps published by S. Augustus Mitchell in 1846. It was one or more of these Mitchell maps which Young ordered from St. Louis during January 1846, as cited previously. The map in question was probably the one entitled, "A New Map of Texas, Oregon, and California," which was 20″ by 22″ and appeared in four colors.[14] (A copy of this map appears on pp. 98-99.) It would seem then that the maps which hung on the walls of the temple, besides Frémont's, were surely Mitchell's, Wilkes', Bonneville's, and most likely Long's. Unfortunately none of the copies used by the Pioneers has survived. Their discovery, especially if they showed Clayton's jottings, would be an invaluable find.

It is interesting to speculate how these guides, travel books and maps might have influenced Clayton in the production of his guide and what he borrowed from others. Probably the earliest publications (not necessarily the earliest publications he saw, however) which might have benefited Clayton were Lewis', Brackenridge's, and Overton and Johnson's tables of distances, and "notes." And certainly the additional information about the trail, grass, water, wood, temperature, landmarks and camping sites which Clayton probably observed in some of the works of Long, Bonneville, Dodge, Townsend, and De Smet would have suggested what a satisfactory trail guide must offer. Some of the few things Clayton could have learned from Hastings and Shively, among others, were totally ignored. He gave no advice whatsoever about pre-emigration preparation, equipment or supplies. Likewise he presented almost nothing regarding relations with Indians.

It is also interesting to examine the contacts the Mormons might have made while on the Missouri River from June 1846 to April 1847 and also along the trail. Surely they talked with all the frontiersmen and Indian agents they could find. From various sources we know they met Robert B. Mitchell, the Indian agent who was located at present-day Council Bluffs, Iowa; with Peter A. Sarpy, another agent at the same place; with a fur trapper named Fontenelle — probably a son of Lucian, who had died in 1840;[15] with the Potawattomi chief, Le Clerk; and with Big Elk of the Omahas.

We also know Young, at least, talked with Father Pierre Jean De Smet while the latter was returning to St. Louis from Oregon. "Mr. Smith," Young recorded on Nov. 19, 1846, "a Catholic priest and missionary to the Black Feet Indians, called on me."[16] Possibly, but highly unlikely, the Mormons may have been familiar with De Smet's 1843 publication, *Letters and Sketches With a Narrative of a Year's Residence* . . . [in] *the Rocky Mountains.* Of this visit De Smet later recorded in his 1847 *Oregon Missions,* "I was presented to their [the Mormons'] president, Mr. Young, a kind and polite gentleman [even though Young, like most Mormons, found it difficult to address him as "Father" and could not even spell his Belgian name correctly!] and he pressed me very earnestly to remain a few days, an invitation which my limited time did not permit me to accept."

Five days later Justin Grosclaude, a fur trader of Swiss ancestry for the American Fur Company, also called on Young and "sketched with pencil a map of the country west of the Missouri and north of the Ponca above the Yellowstone"[17]— a map which, regrettably, has not survived.

On the trail the Mormons likewise made the best use of every opportunity to learn from others. According to Clayton's journal (not *Guide),* on April 17 they met some traders from the Pawnee Village; on May 4 some traders, including Joseph or Lewis Papin from Fort Laramie; and on June 2 "Mr. Bordeau, the principal officer" at Fort Laramie. Also on June 2 they consulted with the guide of a "Missouri Company." On June 9 they met other traders who told them of a skin boat which they had left on the Platte; on the 26th they encountered "a small party of men direct from Oregon"; and on the 27th they met with Maj. Moses (Black) Harris, the first of three important "mountain men" they would encounter. The next day they ran into Jim Bridger and the two parties camped together on the Sandy. Although Bridger was "likered up," they learned much from him. (Incidentally, when "Ol' Gabe" saw Frémont's maps he did not think much of them, for "he knew only the plain traveled road."[18] This was a reference to the strip-like nature of Frémont's maps.)

On June 30 the Pioneers met one of their own, Samuel Brannan, who as noted earlier had reprinted most of the Hastings book in his *New York Messenger* and who in 1846 had led a party of Mormons from New York via Cape Horn to present-day San Francisco. Brannan, like Hastings, was smitten with California's potential and had ridden east via the California Trail and Fort Hall (not via Hastings' "direct route") to try and persuade Young to settle in California. Somehow Brannan had acquired from Hastings "a sketch of the Hastings Cutoff" and "Hastings' directions from Bridger's Fort to the settlements in California, also a map of the route."[19] Very likely Brannan, who may have met Hastings in New York City, had been with him again in California. The two men were alike in that they perceived a great future for themselves in California, but neither realized their dreams.

Finally, on July 10, they met Miles Goodyear who had settled in the Bear River Valley. Goodyear apparently drew for them a map of the route to his settlement.

Enroute Clayton and others checked their findings against their Frémont-Preuss maps. Perhaps it should be noted that the Frémont and Pioneer routes were on opposite banks of the Platte from Grand Island west to Fort Laramie. From Fort Laramie to Fort Bridger they were virtually identical. The Exodus commenced April 5 and by the 28th the Pioneers were opposite the place where Frémont reached the Platte, near the downstream end of Grand Island. On May 7 Orson Pratt was pleased that his longitudinal reading of 100 degrees, 5 minutes, 45 seconds "differed only 2″" or 10 rods [165 feet] from Frémont's longitudinal [measurement] on the other shore of the Platte." Pratt's latitude was given as 40 degrees, 51 minutes, 18 seconds.[20]

On May 18, near present-day Ogallala, Nebraska, Clayton noted that they had reached the Cedar Bluff "as named by Frémont." Here Clayton was using the Frémont-Preuss map of 1843 for it is the only Frémont map which shows the Cedar Bluffs. Today these bluffs, on the Oregon Trail on the south side of the Platte, have been largely inundated by Lake McConaughy. On that same day Clayton was asked to trace the Pioneer route onto one of Frémont's maps, a task he never completed. Two days later he suggested that someone cross the Platte to check out a place noted on Frémont's map as

"Ash Creek [Ash Hollow]," that they might "have a better privilege of testing Fremont's distance [of 132 miles] to Laramie." Two days later they tested their maps against Chimney Rock.

At Fort Laramie on June 2 Clayton compared Frémont's altitude against Pratt's calculation and found Frémont's was 380 feet higher.

On June 5 Clayton passed the Warm Springs as "noted by Fremont", and on June 8 a stream "named on Frémont's map as La Bonte River." The final reference to Frémont in Clayton's journal was made on June 26 while at South Pass: "Fremont represents that he did not discover the highest point on account of the ascent being so gradual. . . ."

Thomas Bullock, the official Clerk of Camp, also made a few references in his own journal to the maps the Pioneers had. Once he found a "river about 10 rods wide" not shown on their maps. Once he "inked our route on a map." That particular map evidently has not survived. Bullock was asked several times to make tracings of parts of Frémont's maps. His most interesting and important journal entry, however, is dated June 30 at Green River when he wrote, "I have eight sections of map to copy." This seems very much like a reference to the Frémont-Pruess map of seven sections.

Surely the Pioneers would have taken with them maps other than those of Frémont-Preuss. Yet I have found but two references to other maps. One is a Clayton reference to the pencil sketch of Grosclaude (see p. 58). The other is a reference to "distances according to Mitchell's map" from Grand Island to Fort Hall found on the flyleaf of the diary kept by Albert Carrington of the Pioneer camp for Amasa Lyman.[21]

There is one final question remaining in this attempt to place Clayton's *Guide* in its proper perspective: "How was Clayton's work thought of by later writers of similar guides?" Soon after Clayton's *Guide* appeared, two other writers of trail guides paid his work the highest of all praise — they plagiarized from him. In 1849 Joseph E. Ware brought out *The Emigrants' Guide to California*. He admitted it was an armchair job compiled "from various sources, private and public, that were known to be reliable." Without further acknowledgment he abridged pp. 12-18 and 23-24 straight from Clayton — over 500 miles of the trail from Fort Laramie to the Bear River.

Three years later P.L. Platt and N. Slater published their *Traveler's Guide Across the Plains . . . to California*. In the preface they admitted that they had consulted "several of the Guides which were in the market," noting that "the best one we saw was that prepared by Mr. W. Clayton. . . .'' Considering this acknowledgment enough, they proceeded to plagiarize his pp. 5-11 and 17-20.

Further evidence of the quality and preeminence of Clayton's *Guide* appeared that same year of 1852 in Hosea B. Horn's, *Horn's Overland Guide from . . . Council Bluffs to California,* New York. In his preface Horn wrote, "Many works, purporting to be Guides, have been offered to the public, and as many have proved worthless, save one — that of Mr. Clayton. . . .'' While Horn could hardly be accused of plagiarism, his sixty-seven-page guide has a format much like Clayton's and follows him rather closely for thirty-four pages.[22] On Nov. 29, 1852, the weekly *Quincy* (Illinois) *Whig* praised Clayton's *Guide* and disparaged most others as "mere catch pennies.'' These three 1852 references to Clayton's *Guide* may have been the result of the "pirated'' edition of his work, which appeared that year. (See p. 8.)

What then was so attractive about Clayton's *Guide* that he, a member of a not overly favored faith at that time and an unknown neophyte in the field, was plagiarized over the famous Frémont and the older and longer works by Hastings, Palmer, Shively, and others? Perhaps it is because Clayton provided, above all things, conciseness, accuracy, and practicality. He had, furthermore, personally been over the route two times. He did not clutter up his pages with philosophical musings, fine writing, or any personal allusions. He clearly and briefly guided the emigrant from one identifiable feature (especially water sources) to another, giving the carefully measured distances between them and a cumulative list of miles traveled from Winter Quarters on the Missouri River as well as miles remaining to the City of the Great Salt Lake. His measurement of distances is his single most important contribution.

Topographic discription and accurate distances, especially in relation to water sources, were essential to any guide to anywhere. Perhaps this came instinctively to Clayton. In any event he tried hard to name many land and water features. Where possible Clayton used the Frémont-Preuss maps and what oral information he could pick up along the way. Sometimes the Pioneers made up names as they went along — some still endure — and sometimes Clayton merely refers to a stream or a lake without citing a name.

By his careful measurements and his recording of toponyms Clayton made a significant contribution to what has come to be called The Great Reconnaissance of the Far West. As stated earlier, it is only in two aspects that his is inferior to many others — he gave no advice on preparing to go west or on how to protect emigrants from Indians.

In keeping with the spirit of Clayton I have attempted to add further identifying comments regarding some topographic features and, where possible, to give the Indian, Spanish, and French name variants. Unless otherwise noted the toponyms used by Clayton remain the same today. Some land features in the *Guide* either no longer exist or cannot now be identified. This is particularly true of certain water sources such as Long, Willow and Ptah lakes, Bluff Springs, as well as Black, Mud, Picanninni, Goose, Duck, Weed, Crooked, Camp, Pond, Watch, and Carrion creeks. Some of them came and went at the whim of the river, marshy soil, poor drainage, flood control and irrigation projects. No reference is made in the notes to these unidentifiable places.

For all the popularity and excellence of Clayton's *Guide* there is no evidence that it was ever reprinted by himself or his church during his lifetime. As Professor Allen has noted, however, a pirated version did appear in 1852. (Council Bluffs had become a favored jumping-off place by 1852 — someone obviously saw the chance to make a good profit from the piracy.) The book was reprinted in 1897 by the Mormons for its historical value, and again in 1930 as a facsimile addendum to Volume Three of B.H. Roberts' *A Comprehensive History of the Church of Jesus Christ of Latter-day Saints*, Salt Lake City, 1930. Since then there have been several other facsimile publications. In 1962 the Daughters of Utah Pioneers issued one and in 1968 so did the Laramie County Library in Cheyenne, Wyoming. In 1974 Ye Galleon Press of Fairfield, Washington, issued a limited edition of 300 copies; that same year University Microfilms offered it as part of the American Culture Series, and in 1976 the Lost Cause Press of Louisville, Kentucky, brought it out in microfiche. More recently the *Guide* appeared as an appendix to Joseph E. Brown and Dan Guravich's *The Mormon Trek West*, Doubleday, 1980. But none of these reprint versions has the thorough annotation and comprehensive biography of the author as this work carries.

As already noted Clayton kept a journal of The Exodus from Nauvoo to the Valley of the Great Salt Lake and back to the Mormon Winter Quarters on the Missouri River. Since its publication in 1921 as *William Clayton's Journal; A Daily Record of the Journey of the Original Company of "Mormon" Pioneers from Nauvoo, Illinois, to the Valley of the Great Salt Lake* it has become the most famous of all Mormon trail journals. So closely are the *Journal* and the *Guide* interrelated that in my notes I have cross-referenced the reader to the *Journal,* appearing at the start of each section of notes. The first set of page numbers and dates refers to the trip west, the second set to the return trip east. This *Journal* has been reprinted but once, by the Taylor Publishing Company of Dallas, in 1973.

For those who may wish to read other contemporary accounts of the Pioneer Trek of 1847 the following printed works are recommended. "Orson Pratt's Journal," *Millennial Star,* vols. 11 and 12, 1849-1850; "Erastus Snow's Journal," *Improvement Era,* vols. 14 and 15, 1911-1912; Howard R. Egan, *Pioneering the West,* Salt Lake City, 1917; *William Clayton's Journal,* Salt Lake City, 1921, reprinted 1973; Andrew Jenson's *Day by Day With the Pioneers, 1847,* Salt Lake City, n.d. (1930?); "The Pioneer Journal of Heber C. Kimball," *Utah Genealogical and Historical Magazine,* vols. 30 and 31, 1939-1940; *Autobiography of Pioneer John Brown,* Salt Lake City, 1941; Leland H. Creek, "Journey to Zion: From the Journal of Erastus Snow," *Utah Humanities Review,* April, July 1946; Maybelle Harmon Anderson, ed., *Appleton Harmon Goes West,* Berkeley, Cal., 1946; "Biography and Diary of Lorenzo Dow Young," *Utah Historical Quarterly,* vol. 14, 1946; Preston Nibley, *Exodus to Greatness,* Salt Lake City, 1947; Matthias F. Cowley, ed., *Wilford Woodruff . . .,* Salt Lake City, 1964; Juanita Brooks, ed., *On the Mormon Frontier: The Diary of Hosea Stout, 1844-61,* 2 vols., Salt Lake City, 1964; Eldon J. Watson, ed., *Manuscript History of Brigham Young, 1846-47,* Salt Lake City, 1971; Stanley B. Kimball and Hal Knight, *111 Days to Zion,* Salt Lake City, 1978.

For those who today may wish to follow the wagon ruts of Clayton, the following publications are recommended. (Those strictly pertinent to the Oregon Trail will be helpful for only 397 miles of Wyoming, between Forts Laramie and Bridger.) Irene D. Paden, *The Wake of the Prairie Schooner,* 1943; R.E. Harvey, "The Mormon Trek Across Iowa Territory," *Annals of Iowa,* July 1946; Margaret Long, *The Oregon Trail,* 1954; Wallace Stegner, *The Gathering of Zion,* 1964; Merrill J. Mattes, *The Great Platte River Road,* 1968; Stanley B. Kimball, "The Iowa Trek of 1846," *The Ensign,* June 1972; William E. Lass, *From the Missouri to the Great Salt Lake,* 1972; Stanley B. Kimball and Hal Knight, *111 Days to Zion,* 1978; *The Mormon Trail: A Study Report,* Heritage Conservation and Recreation Service, 1978; Gregory M. Franzwa, *The Oregon Trail Revisited,* 3rd ed., 1983; Stanley B. Kimball, *Discovering Mormon Trails,* 1979; Joseph E. Brown and Dan Guravich, *The Mormon Trek West,* 1980; Stanley B. Kimball, *The Travelers' Guide to Historic Mormon America,* 13th ed., 1981; Stanley B. Kimball, "The Mormon Trail Network in Iowa, 1838-1863," *BYU Studies,* August 1981;

Aubrey L. Haines, *Historic Sites Along the Oregon Trail,* 2nd ed., 1983; Gregory M. Franzwa, *Maps of the Oregon Trail,* 1982. Although not yet published, regrettably, Olga Sharp Steele's "Geography of the Mormon Trail Across Nebraska," master's thesis, University of Nebraska, 1933, is invaluable.

I would like to thank Professor James B. Allen for having read the manuscript and for having made helpful suggestions. Dr. Allen is now completing a biography of William Clayton. I also thank my wife Violet for having read all versions. I am also grateful to Charles W. Martin of Omaha for his thoughtful critique of the manuscript. Publication of the historical maps is through the courtesy of the Lovejoy Library, Southern Illinois University at Edwardsville. The map on the endpapers of this book was drafted by Diane Clements, who also executed the reference maps in the back of this volume.

NOTES

[1] All references to Clayton's journal in this study are taken from the printed version published in 1921, reprinted in 1973.

[2] Thomas Bullock's journal, July 3, 1846. Archives, Church of Jesus Christ of Latter-day Saints. Hereafter cited as Church Archives.

[3] Clayton's *Guide* is listed in R.F. Perotti and T.N. Luther, *Important Firsts in Missouri Imprints: 1808-58,* Kansas City, 1967.

[4] On June 15, 1850, there is a footnote to Clayton's *Guide* in reference to Salt Lake City. That is all.

[5] The best study of these prophecies and statements is Duane S. Crowther, *The Prophecies of Joseph Smith,* Salt Lake City, 1963, pp. 364-368.

[6] Joseph Smith, *History of the Church,* B.H. Roberts, ed., Salt Lake City, 1950, vol. 6, pp. 275-277, 369-376. Hereafter cited as *HC.*

[7] The *Messenger* was edited by Samuel Brannan who, with official approbation, led a group of Mormons from New York City to California via Cape Horn. They sailed on the *Brooklyn* Feb. 4, 1846, arriving at Yerba Buena (San Francisco) on July 31. Hastings had been lecturing about his new book in New York City and apparently Brannan had met him there. They may have met again in California. See p. 29.

[8] *HC,* vol. 7, pp. 548-558.

[9] Eldon Jay Watson, ed., *Manuscript History of Brigham Young, 1846-1847,* Salt Lake City, 1971, entry of April 4, 1847.

[10] Eugene England, *Brother Brigham,* Salt Lake City, 1980, p. 135.

[11] Credit for unearthing this important letter seems to belong to Dale L. Morgan. It is quoted in Carl I. Wheat's monumental *Mapping the Transmississippi West,* vol. 3, San Francisco, 1959, p. 31, and in Richard H. Jackson's "Myth and Reality: Environmental Perception of the Mormons, 1840-65, An Historical Geosophy," unpublished Ph.D. dissertation, Clark University, 1970, p. 106.

[12] James B. Allen and Glen M. Leonard, *The Story of the Latter-day Saints,* Salt Lake City, 1976, p. 214.

[13] Carleton's logbooks were edited and published by Louis Pelzer as *The Prairie Logbooks,* Chicago, 1943.

[14] In 1827 Martin Harris showed a copy of some Book of Mormon characters to Prof. Charles Anthon of New York City, and to the shadowy "Dr. Mitchell." For many years some Mormons thought that "Dr. Mitchell" and this man might have been the same person. See my "The Anthon Transcript: People, Primary Sources, and Problems," *BYU Studies,* vol. 10 (Spring 1970), pp. 325-352.

[15] The only source I have found for this alleged visit with Fontenelle is the journal of Lorenzo D. Young, Nov. 15, 1846, Church Archives.

[16] *Manuscript History of Brigham Young,* Nov. 19, 1846.

[17] Ibid., Nov. 24, 1846.

[18] Matthias F. Cowley, ed. *Wilford Woodruff,* Salt Lake City, 1909 (reprinted 1964), p. 306.

[19] The source of both sketch and map is Bullock's journal, July 7, 1847.

[20] Orson Pratt's journal, May 7, 1847. This sighting was taken near present-day Gothenberg, Nebraska. It proves that Pratt was reading page 19 of Frémont's 1843 *Report,* where is given this June 18, 1842 reading of 100 degrees, 05 minutes, 47 seconds west longitude.

[21] Wheat, *Mapping the Transmississippi West,* p. 31.

[22] In 1853 Frederick H. Piercy (who in 1855 published his *Route From Liverpool to Salt Lake City)* used both the Clayton and Horn guides.

All photographs by the author unless credited otherwise.

THE

LATTER-DAY SAINTS'

EMIGRANTS' GUIDE:

BEING A

TABLE OF DISTANCES,

SHOWING ALL THE

SPRINGS, CREEKS, RIVERS, HILLS, MOUNTAINS,

CAMPING PLACES, AND ALL OTHER NOTABLE PLACES,

FROM COUNCIL BLUFFS,

TO THE

VALLEY OF THE GREAT SALT LAKE.

ALSO, THE

LATITUDES, LONGITUDES AND ALTITUDES

OF THE PROMINENT POINTS ON THE ROUTE.

TOGETHER WITH REMARKS ON THE NATURE OF THE LAND,
TIMBER, GRASS, &c.

THE WHOLE ROUTE HAVING BEEN CAREFULLY MEASURED BY A ROADOME-
TER, AND THE DISTANCE FROM POINT TO POINT, IN
ENGLISH MILES, ACCURATELY SHOWN.

BY W. CLAYTON.

ST. LOUIS:

MO. REPUBLICAN STEAM POWER PRESS—CHAMBERS & KNAPP,

1848.

PREFACE.

When the author first compiled the following work, it was not with a design to publish it, although well aware of the advantages which emigrants, traveling to the VALLEY OF THE GREAT SALT LAKE, would continually realize by having it in their possession. However, there were so many who applied for copies of it—and the labor of writing a copy being considerable, as well as requiring much time—it was concluded to publish it in its present form, by which means it can be afforded at a price which will bring it within reach of any person wishing to have it.

Many works have been published, and maps exhibited for the instruction of emigrants, but none which ever pretended to set forth the particulars contained in this work, so far as regards the route from Council Bluffs to the Great Salt Lake. The distances from point to point are shown as near as a *Roadometer* can measure; and by this means the traveler can know, each day, the kind of country lying before him, and how far he must go in order to find a suitable place to camp at night.

Emigrants have lost many of their teams in the neighborhood of the *Alkali lakes*, in consequence of not knowing the distance from any one of these lakes to good water. By paying attention to the *remarks* in this work, a person need run *no risk*, inasmuch as all the Alkali lakes, which are near the road, are mentioned—and, also, the places where an encampment can be formed with safety.

The author feels a delicacy in saying much in favor of the " *Guide*," but is well aware that, when its merits have been tested by experience, no person will repent of having purchased it. It is, therefore, submitted cheerfully to the consideration of an intelligent public.

AUTHOR.

St. Louis, Mo., 13th *March,* 1848.

4

EXPLANATION.

~~~~~~~~~~~~~~~~

In the following table, the *large type* shows the prominent points and places which will naturally be noticed by the emigrant. The *first* column of figures shows the distance from point to point, in English miles. The *second* column of figures shows the total distance of each point to Winter Quarters; and the, *third* column, the total distance of each point to the Temple Block, in the City of the Great Salt Lake. As, for example:

How far is it from Winter Quarters to Pappea?
Answer. (page 5, second line) 18 miles.
How far from Pappea to the Elk Horn river?
Answer. (page 5, second and third lines) 9 miles, &c.
Again: How far is it from Raw Hide Creek to Fort John?
Answer. (page 11, last line) 12 miles.
How far is Fort John from Winter Quarters?
Answer. (p. 12, first line) 522 miles.
How far is Fort John from the City of the Great Salt Lake?
Answer. (p. 12, third column of figures) 509 miles.

The *small type*, in this table, contains the various *remarks* touching the nature of the road, lands, and its adaptation for camping purposes, &c. For example:

What is said concerning the " La Bonte river?" Page 13, second line.

Answer. "It is a good place to camp—being plenty of timber, grass and water"—the necessaries for camping purposes, and consequently can be depended on. But, if thought advisable to go a little further, " there is a good camping place a mile further," consequently you have choice of the two good places, within one mile of each other.

What is said of a branch of the La, Bonte? Page 13, third line.

Answer. " Doubtful about water;" consequently not safe to depend on for a camp ground. It is also said that the " banks are steep," which shows that it is not very good to cross, &c.

5

EMIGRANTS' GUIDE.

PROMINENT POINTS AND REMARKS.	Dist. miles.	From W Qrs. miles.	From C of G S L miles.
Winter Quarters, Lat. 41° 18′ 53″ -			1031
The road good, but very crooked, following the ridges and passing over a continual succession of hills and hollows.			
Pappea, ten feet wide, high banks. -	18	18	1013
Some timber on the creek, but it is difficult to water teams. After this, the road is crooked and uneven to the Elk Horn.			
Elk Horn, nine rods wide, three feet deep.	9	27	1004
Current rather swift, and not very pleasant to ferry. Plenty of timber on its banks. (See Note 1.)			
Creek, ten feet wide, steep banks. -	¾	27¾	1003¼
This creek has a good bridge over it, but little timber on the banks. There is a high post, erected near the bridge, for a guide to it.			
Platte river and Liberty Pole. - -	11¼	39	992
Plenty of timber, but you will probably have to go to the river for water—distance about a quarter of a mile The nearest and best road to water is round the east point of the timber.			
Small Lake (narrow) south side the road.	3¼	42¼	988½
No timber on the Lake.			
Circular Lake, or pond, close to the road, (south.) - - - - -	¾	43¼	987¾
No timber. In the neighborhood of this, the road runs alongside a number of small lakes, or ponds, for two miles; but there is little timber near them.			
R. R. and T., road joins the river, Lat. 41° 27′ 5″ - - - - -	9	52¼	978¾
This is a point where a branch of the river runs round an island, on which is plenty of timber. Not much water in the channel, but plenty for camping purposes.			
Indian Grave, north side the road. -	7½	59¾	971¼
This is a large pile of earth, about eighty yards north of the road			
R. R. and T., road joins the river. -	½	60¼	970¾
Plenty of timber and water, without leaving the road			
Shell creek, 12 feet wide, three feet deep.	2	62¼	968¾
This creek is bridged, and a few rods lower is a place to ford Plenty of timber on it. After this you will probably find no water for twelve miles, without turning considerably from the road.			
Small lake, south side of the road. -	5¾	68	963
Plenty of water in the Spring season, but none in Summer. It was entirely dry, October 18, 1847.			

See Map Section A, Page 88

Compare Clayton's *Journal,* pp. 78-84, Apr. 14-19; pp. 375-376, Oct. 18-21.

WINTER QUARTERS. This was the main Mormon encampment during 1836-48. It was on the west side of the Missouri River in an area now known as Florence, a suburb in the northern portion of Omaha. The good road was the well-traveled route of traders to and from the Pawnee villages on the Loup River, about 120 miles west of Winter Quarters. The astronomical sightings were made by Apostle Orson Pratt.

PAPPEA. Properly this was the Big Papillion or Butterfly River, so named from the masses of butterflies once found on its banks. The name of this first topographic feature on the Mormon Trail suggests the influence of the French *coureurs de bois* and *voyageurs* in the exploration and topography of the West since at least the 1680s and up until 1763. Then the French empire in the New World, from the Alleghenies to the Rocky Mountains, was lost to the English and Spanish.

ELK HORN. This river was known as *Watatungya* to the Otoes, *Quigitic* to the Pawnees, and *Corne de Cerf* to the French. While the original crossing of April 1847 appears to have been about one mile south of today's Waterloo, Clayton's reference here seems to be about five miles north, just west of today's Elk City, and more directly west of Winter Quarters. The creek three-quarters of a mile farther was probably the Rawhide.

LIBERTY POLE. This was a forty-foot tall cottonwood pole, flying a white flag, erected on June 14, 1847 by the Second Company of Mormons, which followed the Pioneers by about two months. (Clayton first noted it on his return trip from the Valley of the Great Salt Lake.) This first marker on the great trail marked the staging ground of the Pioneers and was about a quarter-mile from the Platte River southwest of Fremont, perhaps in Sec. 21, T17N, R8W. It was gradually covered with names as far up as emigrants could reach and was still in place at least as late as 1857.

LAKES. These are now part of the Fremont State Recreation Area.

R. R. AND T. These initials, used occasionally by Clayton, stand for the availability of Road, River and Timber. Many islands were made and unmade by the vagaries of the Platte River.

INDIAN GRAVE. This could have been Otoe or Omaha, but probably it was a Pawnee grave; certainly not the scaffold type burial of the Sioux. Clayton refers to the Pawnees five times in three pages and then never again refers to or gives advice about Indians. The Pioneers subsequently met many Sioux, Crow, Snake and Great Basin Indians. This is a serious omission in his guide.

SHELL CREEK. Some maps called it the Mussel Shell; to the French it was *La Petite Coquille*. The Pawnee nation, centered on the Loup River, routinely extracted tolls here. The bridge was pre-Mormon, built by Indian traders.

SMALL LAKE. The date of October 18, 1847, of course, is in reference to the return from the valley.

The Elkhorn River, first major obstacle west of Winter Quarters, is shown about where the Pioneers crossed it in 1847.

6

PROMINENT POINTS AND REMARKS.	DIST. miles.	FROM W' QRS. miles.	From C of G S L miles.
R. and R., road joins the river. - - After this point you will have four or five miles of heavy, sandy road.	6½	74½	956½
Long Lake, south side the road. - - There is a little timber where this lake joins the river, and it is a good camping place.	½	75	956
Forks of road to new and old Pawnee villages. - - - - - - The left hand road leads to the Pawnee location of 1847; the other to the old village. The latter is your route.	5½	80½	950½
Lake, south of the road. - - - Plenty of timber close to the road. The banks of the lake are high, but there is a small pond near, where teams can water.	½	81	950
Loup Fork—lake and timber. - - Opposite to where the Pawnees were located, in the Spring of 1847, and is a good place to camp	5	86	945
Lake and timber, south of the road. -	8¼	94¼	936¾
Looking-glass creek, 16 feet wide, 2 deep. There is a poor bridge over this creek. It is, however, not difficult to ford. Plenty of timber on and near it.	1	95¼	935¾
Long Lake, south side the road. - - Some timber on the south bank, but none on the north side.	2	97¼	933¾
Beaver river, 25 feet wide, 2 feet deep: Lat. 41° 25′ 13″; Long. 98° 0′ 15″. Plenty of good timber on both sides. There are two fording places. The upper one is good going in, but steep on the opposite side. The lower one not good going down, but good on the other side.	6½	103¾	927¼
Plumb creek, five feet wide: Lat. 41° 24′ 29″; Altitude, 1,090 feet. - - On this creek the old Pawnee mission station stands, but is not a very good place to camp, being near the Pawnee cornfields. The creek was dry, October 16, 1847.	6¾	110½	920½
Ash creek, 12 feet wide, one foot deep. Some timber, but not a very good chance to camp.	2½	113	918
Ford of the Loup Fork: Lat. 41° 22′ 37″; Long. 98° 11′ 0″. - - - - This is the pioneer's ford, but is considered not so good as the upper ford. River about 300 yards wide.	1¼	114¼	916¾
Old Pawnee village. - - - - - Formerly occupied by the Grand Pawnee and Tappas bands; but burned by the Sioux, in the Fall of 1846.	½	114¾	916¼
Cedar creek, 8 rods wide, 2 feet deep. - Some timber, and plenty of willow. After this, the road runs on the bottom, through high grass for some distance, and gradually rises to higher land.	1½	116¼	914¾
Road descends to low-land again. - You will now find some deep ravines to cross, but none difficult.	3	119¼	911¾
Road leaves the river, and turns up a ravine. After ascending the higher land, the road is good and level, except crossing the deep, dry ravines.	1¾	121	910
Road descends into a ravine. - - You travel up this ravine a quarter of a mile, mostly through high grass.	½	121½	909½

See Map Section B, Page 88

Compare *Journal,* pp. 85-103, April 20-25; pp. 333-375, Oct. 15-17.

LONG LAKE. This was a lake made and unmade by the Platte.

FORKS OF ROAD. The center of the Pawnee nation was along the Loup River. In 1820 Major Long found three villages in one ten-mile stretch along the north bank of the Loup. In 1844 Lieutenant Carleton noted but one, near present-day Fullerton, at the mouth of Cedar Creek. This "old" village was burned by the Sioux in 1846, and the Pawnees relocated south of the Loup, just west of present-day Columbus. This village became the "new" one or the "Pawnee location of 1847."

LOUP FORK. This river derives its name either from the wolves found by the French in the area or from the French translation of the name of one band of Pawnees, the Skidi.

LOOKING GLASS CREEK. On some early maps it is called the Grape Creek. To the Pawnee it was *Quitooquataleri,* or Water That Reflects Your Shadow. The creek has changed its course some since 1847 and no longer runs so clear.

LAKE. This is probably one of the lakes near present-day Pawnee Park in Columbus.

BEAVER RIVER. To the Pawnee this river was called *Quitpisa-nontch.* It is located at present-day Genoa, which was founded by the Mormons in 1857 as a way station. Pratt's longitudinal reading is off by 14 minutes or nearly twelve miles too far west. The two fords were one mile apart. They were immediately south of Genoa in Sections 13 and 24.

PLUMB CREEK. The mission to the Pawnees was abandoned after the Sioux raid of 1846 and the missionaries transferred to Bellevue on the Missouri River. The name of the creek comes from the wild plums which grew on its banks.

ASH CREEK. The Pioneers actually crossed Cedar River. Ash Creek is a tributary which flows into the Cedar several miles north of the trail.

FORD OF THE LOUP. The Loup River was a dangerous one. The Pioneer ford probably was just east of Fullerton in Sec. 4, T16N, R5W. The returning or "upper" ford which Clayton recommended was upstream, near Sec. 14, T15N, R8W, about three miles east of Major Long's ford of 1820.

OLD PAWNEE VILLAGE. (See above, "Forks of Road".) Clayton refers to the Grand Pawnee and Tappas (sometimes spelled Tepage) bands. Prior to 1847 two other bands, the Republican Pawnee and Pawnee Loup, had also been in the area.

CEDAR CREEK. On some maps this stream is named Willow Creek.

The Pioneers followed the Platte River system for more than 600 miles. It is still broad, shallow, and has many sand bars. So many, in fact, that westering Americans called it a river which "flowed

ROAD DESCENDS. The Pioneers are still on the north bank of the Loup.

upside down." Emigrants seemed to enjoy insulting this strange stream. It was referred to as being "a mile wide, a foot deep, too thin to plow and too thick to drink."

7

PROMINENT POINTS AND REMARKS.	DIST. miles.	From W Qrs. miles.	From C of G S L miles.
Old Pawnee village, south side the road.	5½	127	904
On the banks of the Loup Fork, but mostly destroyed.			
Road descends from the bluffs. - -	½	127½	903½
After descending here, you cross a creek twelve feet wide, and one foot deep—banks soft, but not difficult. You then travel through high grass and small bushes.			
Road ascends the bluffs. - - - -	¼	127¾	903¼
After traveling about four miles, then turning left from the road, so as to strike the timber you see ahead where it meets the river, the road can be shortened at least a half mile.			
Upper ford of the Loup Fork. - -	6	133¾	897¼
You will find the water in some places near 3 feet deep, and will have to travel down the river about half a mile, to avoid deep holes, and find a good place to get out. (See Note 2.)			
Road ascends the bluffs. - - - -	5¾	139½	891½
After ascending the bluffs you will find a heavy, sandy road for five or six miles.			
Prairie creek, 12 feet wide 1½ feet deep.	18	157½	873½
Plenty of water and grass, but no timber. Banks, some soft and miry. By taking a south-west course from this creek, you would strike Wood river six or eight miles above the old crossing place, and thence crossing to the Platte, by a course a little west of south, the road may be shortened at least five miles.			
Dry creek. - - - - - -	1	158½	872½
" " - - - - - -	½	159	872
Main Platte river. - - - - -	6¾	165¾	865¼
You do not come within two miles of the river, until you arrive at Wood river.			
Wood river, 12 feet wide, one foot deep.	3½	169¼	861¾
Plenty of timber, and a good place to camp. Banks descending, steep, and some soft—but good going out. The road now generally runs from one to two miles distant from the main Platte.			
Road descends to lower land. - -	14	183¼	847¾
The road now runs near the timber for two miles. The grass is high, and a good chance to camp, without turning off the road.			
Road ascends to higher land. - -	2	185¼	845¾
You will probably have to turn off the road some, for the next camping place.			
Deep ravine—steep descent. - -	22¾	208	823
" " - - - - - -	¼	208¼	822¾
Two and a quarter miles beyond this, is a good place to camp, there being plenty of grass and water, on a low bench, about twenty rods south of the road. There is, however, no timber but willow.			
Deep dry creek. - - - - -	3½	211¾	819¼
No timber on it.			
Creek or slough, south side the road. -	1¾	213½	817½
Plenty of willows and grass, but doubtful for water.			
Deep, dry creek. - - - - -	4¼	217¾	813¼
The head of Grand Island is about opposite to this creek, but the road now runs so far from the river, we could not ascertain exactly.			

See Map Section C, Page 88

Compare *Journal*, pp. 103-123, April 26-May 1; pp. 372-376, Oct. 10-14.

OLD PAWNEE VILLAGE. Here were the remains of yet another Pawnee village, this one located west of Fullerton.

UPPER FORD. As already noted, this was probably in Sec. 14, T15N, R8W, and was not used by the westbound Pioneers.

PRAIRIE CREEK. Although completely Americanized, the word is French for meadow. This creek was probably forded in Sec. 22, T13N, R8W. The reference to the "old crossing place" is more evidence that the *Guide* is deviating again from the Pioneer route. From the Loup to the Wood River the Pioneers may have blazed parts of the new road. See also Clayton's Note 2.

MAIN PLATTE RIVER. This sighting of the Platte appears to have been about five miles east of today's city of Grand Island. From here the Pioneers generally followed the Platte River Valley for more than 600 miles to present-day Casper, Wyoming. The Indians, Spanish and French knew this river as the *Nebraska, Chata,* or *La Plat* — all of which mean shallow or flat. The superfluous "te" was added by Americans.

WOOD RIVER. This stream was crossed about 2.5 miles southeast of present-day Alda.

DEEP RAVINES. These ravines were about two miles west of present-day Kearney, Nebraska.

DEEP DRY CREEK. Here the Pioneers first sighted the Grand Island, *La Grande Isle* of the French. Where this island was and how long it was cannot now be determined precisely, because it was and still is constantly being redefined by the river. Most estimates put its length at between forty and sixty miles. Since Frémont, following the Oregon Trail, picked up the Platte Valley opposite its eastern head, the Pioneers could now start checking their positions against the Frémont-Preuss maps they had with them.

8

PROMINENT POINTS AND REMARKS.	Dist. miles.	From W Qrs. miles.	From C of G S L miles.
Elm creek.	3¼	221	810
Deep banks, plenty of timber, but no water, October 9, 1847.			
Road leaves the river near timber.	6¾	227¾	803¼
This is a pretty good camping place.			
Buffalo creek, south side the road.	½	228¼	802¾
A wide creek, with deep banks, but no timber except a few willow bushes. The road runs alongside this creek for three and a half miles.			
Crossing of Buffalo creek.	3	231¾	799¼
R. and R., road runs near the river.	7	239¼	791¾
Pretty good chance to camp.			
R. and R., road runs near the river.	5¼	244½	786½
Plenty of buffalo-grass, and short prairie-grass. Plenty of timber on an island, close by.			
Willow Lake, south of the road.	7	251½	779½
Good place to water teams, but no timber for camping purposes.			
Ptah Lake, south of the road.	7¾	259¼	771¾
The lake is long and very crooked. About a mile before you arrive at it, the road runs near the river a little piece, then leaves it again.			
Deep, dry creek.	2½	261¾	769¼
Low, sandy bluffs, extending to the river.	14	275¾	755¼
R. and R. near the Sandy Bluffs: Latitude 41° 0′ 47″.	3	278¾	752¼
After leaving this place, the road leaves the river, and runs near the foot of the bluffs, to avoid a bad swamp. You will not strike the river for sixteen miles, but will have no difficulty in finding feed and water.			
Skunk creek, six feet wide.	2	280¾	750¼
Crossing of Skunk creek.	5	286¼	744¾
Banks some soft, but not difficult. No timber.			
Lake or marsh, south of the road.	1	287¼	743¾
Lake, south of the road.	1	288¾	742¼
Plenty of grass and water, but no timber nearer than five or six miles.			
Good spring of cold water.	4¼	293	738
At the foot of the bluffs, north of the road, and at the head of the Pawnee swamps.			
Low, sandy bluffs.	1¼	294¼	736¾
This is opposite to the junction of the north and south forks of Platte river. Lat. 41° 7′ 44″; Long. 100° 47′ 15″; Altitude, 2,685 feet.			
Carrion creek, 10 feet wide, one foot deep.	3½	297¾	733¼
Good place for grass, but no timber near.			
R. R. and T., road, river and timber.	4¾	302½	728½
Good place to camp.			
Last timber on north side the river.	3¾	306¼	724¾
You will find no more timber on the north side the river for two hundred miles, except one lone tree. Your only dependence for fuel will be buffalo chips and drift wood.			
Wide, deep creek.	2¼	308½	722½
Plenty of water, October 4, 1847. The banks are high but not bad to cross.			

See Map Section D, Page 89

Compare *Journal,* pp. 123-141, May 1-10; pp. 367-372, Oct. 4-7

ELM CREEK. This crossing is in the present-day community of the same name.

BUFFALO CREEK CROSSING. This site is about two miles east of Overton. The creek may have been named by Heber C. Kimball, one of the Pioneer leaders.

BUFFALO GRASS. In 1847 wood was very scarce along the Platte. Seedlings fell victim to spring floods, prairie fire, and trampling buffalo. Fuel was often obtainable only on river islands, which were also havens during prairie fires. Buffalo grass is a fine, short, nutritious plant.

WILLOW AND PTAH LAKES. These lakes no longer exist; they were made and unmade by the river. ''Ptah'' is surely of Indian origin, not Egyptian.

SKUNK CREEK. This name was given by Heber C. Kimball and is probably today's Pawnee Creek, near Brady's Island.

LOW SANDY BLUFFS. These bluffs commence just west of the present-day city of North Platte. Extending for miles, they come down to the river six times, forming the most difficult portion of the Mormon Trail in Nebraska. The confluence today of the North and South Platte is at longitude 100 degrees, 40 minutes. Not knowing where it was in 1847, or where the Pioneers thought it was (for it was sometimes difficult to determine), we do not know how accurate Pratt's longitude reading is. The famous roadometer was installed just west of here.

LAST TIMBER. There were at least three different ''Lone Trees'' along the Mormon Trail. This one was located at Cedar Grove, two miles east of and opposite Ash Hollow.

9

PROMINENT POINTS AND REMARKS.	DIST. miles.	From W QRS. miles.	From C of G S L miles.
R. R. and lake, road and river near a bayou. Opposite to this place are several islands, covered with willow bushes, which will answer for fuel, and there is little difficulty in getting to it.	1¼	309¾	721¼
Black mud creek. - - - - - Plenty of water, October 3, 1847, but little feed for teams.	2	311¾	719¼
R. and R., road joins the river. - - After this, the road again leaves the river, until you arrive at the north Bluff Fork. Road good, but poor feed.	2	313¾	717¼
Small creek. - - - - - - Steep banks, but very little water.	3½	317¼	713¾
North Bluff Fork, 6 rods wide, 2 feet deep. Swift current, muddy water, low banks, quick-sand bottom, but not bad to cross. Poor place for grass.	3½	320¾	710¼
Sandy Bluffs, east foot. - - - The road over these bluffs is very crooked, but not bad. If a road can be made up the bed of the river, it would save at least two miles travel.	1½	322¼	708¾
Sandy Bluffs, west foot. - - - - By following the foot of the bluffs, after this, the road may be shortened at least a mile, and be equally as good a road as to follow the river.	4½	326¾	704¼
2d. Sandy Bluffs, east foot. - - - These bluffs are hard on teams, being mostly soft sand.	4	330¾	700¼
2d. Sandy Bluffs, west foot. - -	1¼	332	699
Bluff Creek, 4 feet wide, 1 foot deep. - After this, the road may be made considerably shorter, by following the foot of the bluffs.	¼	332¼	698¾
3d. Sandy Bluffs, east foot. - - - These bluffs are sandy, and heavy on teams. Near the west side you will find several steep places to descend, but not difficult, the sand being soft.	6¼	338½	692½
Small creek, running between the bluffs. Many small Lizards on the sandy places, but they appear to be perfectly harmless.	¼	338¾	692¼
Sandy Bluffs, west foot. - - - -	2	340¾	690¼
Bluff Spring and small creek 200 yards, and one a quarter of a mile. - - In the neighborhood of these creeks the land is swampy and soft. The road was made close to the bluffs, to avoid the swamps.	¼	341	690
Petite creek, 4 feet wide, 9 inches deep. Plenty of water, some muddy, October 1, 1847. Latitude 41° 12′ 50″.	1	342	689
Picanninni creek, 3 feet wide. - - Good spring water, and plentiful, October 1. 1847.	1¼	343¼	687¾
Goose creek, 30 feet wide, 3 inches deep. After crossing this, you pass over a low range of bluffs, very sandy, but only a quarter of a mile wide; then you descend on the bottom land again, but will find it soft and springy.	¾	344	687
Small spring creek. - - - - - Many springs of cold water at the foot of the bluffs.	1¼	345¼	685¾
Small creek, 4 feet wide. - - - Plenty of clear cold water, October 1, 1847.	1¼	346½	684½

See Map Section E, Page 89

Compare *Journal,* pp. 141-151, May 10-15; pp. 368-369, Oct. 1-3.

R.R. AND LAKE. Sometimes these islands offered only willows and bushes for fuel. The most important source of fuel to the Pioneers was, of course, dried buffalo dung or "chips."

NORTH BLUFF FORK. This is today's Birdwood Creek.

SANDY BLUFFS. From here, west of Sutherland, the bluffs became increasingly difficult to travel. The worst seem to have been in Sections 3 and 4, T14N, R33W, immediately north of Sutherland when they came to the river for the first time. Here may be found some of the best preserved Mormon Trail ruts in Nebraska.

An aerial view of the sand hill ruts, some of the best Mormon Trail remnants in Nebraska.

10

PROMINENT POINTS AND REMARKS.	DIST. miles.	From W QRS. miles.	From C of G S L miles.
Duck-weed creek, 10 feet wide.	¼	346¾	684¼
Abundance of good, cold spring water, Oct. 1, 1847.			
Shoal stream, 3 feet wide.	2	348¾	682¼
Dry, October 1, 1847.			
Rattlesnake creek, 20 feet wide, 1½ ft. deep.	3¾	352½	678½
Swift current, sandy bottom, but not bad to cross.			
Cedar Bluffs.	1½	354	677
On the south side the river. Lat. 41° 13′ 44″ Long. 101° 52′			
Creek, six feet wide.	5	359	672
Water plenty, September 30, 1847. Land, in this neighborhood, sandy.			
Creek, four feet wide.	½	359½	671½
Plenty of water, September 30, 1847.			
Crooked Creek, five feet wide.	¼	359¾	671¼
Plenty of water, September 30, 1847.			
Camp Creek, eight feet wide.	4	363¾	667¼
Two creeks here, about the same size, but a few rods apart—water cold and plenty, September 30, 1847. No doubt they rise from springs.			
Creek, three feet wide.	4	367¾	663¼
Plenty of water, May 20, but dry, September 30, 1847.			
Pond Creek, four feet wide.	¼	368	663
Dry, September 30, near the river, but further north many ponds and tall grass.			
Wolf Creek, 20 feet wide.	1½	369½	661½
At the east foot of Sandy Bluffs, which are bad to cross, you will probably have to double teams, if heavy loaded.			
Sandy Bluffs, west foot.	¾	370¼	660¾
Two hundred yard further, is a creek five feet wide.			
Watch Creek, 8 feet wide, and 2 feet deep.	3½	373¾	657¼
After this, the road runs pretty near the river banks, to avoid some swamps near the bluffs.			
"Lone Tree," north side the river.	4¼	378	653
About three hundred yards south from the road.			
Ash Hollow, south side the river.	2¾	380¾	650¼
So named from a grove of Ash timber growing on it. It occupies a space of about fifteen or twenty acres, and is surrounded by high bluffs.			
Castle Creek, 6 rods wide, 2 feet deep.	3	383¾	647¼
Swift current, quick-sand bottom, water muddy. Low banks, but not good to cross, on account of quick-sands.			
Castle Bluffs, south side the river.	4¼	388	643
You cross no more creeks of water, until you arrive at Crab creek, twenty-five and a half miles from here. The road good, except in one place, where you travel three-fourths of a mile over sand.			
Sand Hill creek, 12 feet wide, south side the road.	¾	388¾	642¼
Near some sandy mounds, on the north side the road			
Creek or slough.	1½	390¼	640¾
Dry.			
Creek or slough.	7½	397¾	633¼
Dry.			
Sandy Bluffs, east foot.	3	400¾	630¼

See Map Section F, Page 89

Compare *Journal,* pp. 151-168, May 16-21; pp. 366-368, Sept. 26-30.

RATTLESNAKE CREEK. This stream was named by Brigham Young and is probably today's Whitetail Creek.

CEDAR BLUFFS. These bluffs, on the south side or Oregon Trail, were noted in the preface. They were the first topographic feature the Pioneers checked against the Frémont-Preuss maps. They were north of present-day Brule. Today this feature is largely inundated by Lake McConaughy, which covers twenty-four miles of the trail northwest of Ogallala. This longitude reading seems to be accurate.

LONE TREE. This was one of three trees so named along the Mormon Trail. It was a Cedar Tree and stood three miles east of present-day Lewellen. Some Pioneers, including Young, carved their initials on its trunk, thereby contributing to its demise.

ASH HOLLOW. The Frémont-Preuss map cited it as Ash Creek and to the French it was (rather poetically) *Coulée des Frênes* (A Flowing of Ash Trees). It was a famous stopping place on the Oregon Trail and is now part of the Ash Hollow State Historical Park. At Clayton's suggestion some Mormons crossed over to determine whether it really was Ash Creek, so they could check their position against the Frémont maps.

CASTLE CREEK. This is today's Blue Creek.

CASTLE BLUFFS. These bluffs on the Oregon Trail were evidence that the Mormons had entered the broken lands of the Upper Missouri Basin. Thereafter the terrain became increasingly more interesting and varied. For eighty miles to Scotts Bluffs the Pioneers traveled what might loosely be called a monument valley. Clayton thought Castle Bluffs looked like a ruined castle he remembered in Lancaster, England.

11

PROMINENT POINTS AND REMARKS.	DIST. miles.	From W QRS. miles.	From C of G S L miles.
Sandy Bluffs, west foot. - - -	½	401¼	629¾
Dry creek. - - - - - -	¼	401½	629½
Dry do. - - - - - -	¾	402¼	628¾
Dry creek, 30 feet wide. - - -	4	406¼	624¾
The road runs near the river, from here to Crab creek.			
Crab Creek, 20 feet wide, very shoal. -	3	409¼	621¾
Two miles further you will see some high bluffs on the right. By ascending one of the highest you will see Chimney Rock, to the west.			
Small lake, south of the road. - -	1¼	410½	620½
Good chance to camp, without turning from the road.			
Cobble Hills, east foot. - - -	5	415½	615½
You cross three dry creeks before you arrive here. and then you travel over another range of sandy bluffs—ascent pretty steep, but not very sandy.			
Cobble Hills, west foot. - - -	2¼	417¾	613¼
After you descend on the low land, you will find it mostly sandy for ten miles, and in some places very heavy drawing.			
"Ancient Bluff Ruins," north side the road. Latitude 41° 33′ 3″. - - -	1¼	419	612
Resembling the ruins of ancient castles, fortifications, &c.; but visitors must be cautious, on account of the many rattle-snakes lurking round, and concealed in the clefts of the bluffs.			
R. and R., road joins the river. - -	10½	429½	601½
Good place to camp. After this, the road runs near the river, until you arrive at the next low sandy ridges.			
Low sandy bluffs, east foot. - -	7½	437	594
Low sandy bluffs, west foot. - -	1	438	593
After this, the land for several miles, is soft in wet weather, but good traveling in dry weather.			
"Chimney Rock," (meridian) south side the river. - - - - -	14½	452½	578½
The higher land now begins to be sandy and barren. Many Prickly-pears and Wild Sage, which continue mostly through the remainder of the journey.			
Scott's Bluffs, (mer.) south side the river.	19½	472	559
The road here is near enough to the river to camp Lat. of meridian. 41° 50′ 52″.; Long. 103° 20′.			
Spring Creek, 10 feet wide, 8 inches deep.	4	476	555
South of the road. You do not cross it, but travel half a mile alongside. Good water, and many trout in it.			
R. and R., road runs near the river. -	12½	488½	542½
Good chance to camp.			
Low sandy bluffs, north side the road. -	2¾	491¼	539¾
You travel at the foot of these bluffs, but will find the road sandy and heavy on teams.			
Creek, about 200 yards south of road. -	2	493¼	537¾
By ascending one of the highest bluffs near, you have a view of "Laramie Peak" in the Black Hills.			
Timber, north side the river. - -	11½	504¾	526¼
Road here about a quarter of a mile from the river—after this, generally from one to two miles distant. The road, to Laramie, very sandy.			
"Raw Hide" creek, 1 rod wide. : -	5¼	510	521
Plenty of water, June 1st, but dry, Sept. 15, 1847.			

See Map Section G, Page 89-90

Compare *Journal,* pp. 169-208, May 22-June 1; pp. 362-365, Sept. 15-25.

DRY CREEK. Perhaps this is the same one shown on a Frémont-Preuss map.

CRAB CREEK. This stream at present-day Lisco was named by the Mormons. The "high bluffs" two miles west are known today by some as Indian Lookout Point. This is the first dramatic topographic feature along the Mormon Trail from Nauvoo. Chimney Rock is the single most famous topographic feature on either the Oregon or Mormon Trails. To the Mormons it was another check on their maps. Although sixty-three miles short of the fact, the Saints came to consider it halfway between the Missouri River and the Great Salt Lake.

COBBLE HILLS. These gravel bluffs, so difficult for oxen to negotiate, were named by the Pioneers and are located between Indian Lookout Point and the Ancient Bluff Ruins.

ANCIENT BLUFF RUINS. These magnificently-eroded formations were named by English Pioneers who thought they resembled ruined castles in their homeland. On Sunday, May 23, the leaders of the Pioneers climbed the highest bluff, wrote their names on a buffalo skull and placed it at the southwest corner. Rattlesnakes were a common danger to Mormon emigrants, but caused few deaths.

CHIMNEY ROCK. At this point the Pioneers were due north of this brule clay and sandstone formation and they judged it to be 260 feet high. Clayton thought it looked like "the large factory chimneys of England." Many an unwary Mormon emigrant learned the hard way about prickley pears.

SCOTTS BLUFF. Although the Pioneers remained north of the Platte all the way to Fort Laramie, later companies of Mormons crossed the river here to the Oregon Trail. The longitude reading, if related correctly by Clayton, is incorrect by about 22 minutes, or nearly nineteen miles to the east.

LOW SANDY BLUFFS. These bluffs are just east of the present-day Wyoming-Nebraska border at Henry. Here, on Sunday, May 30, Young held a special and formal Prayer Circle on behalf of the Pioneers, those following, and others remaining at Winter Quarters.

CREEK. Later that same May 30 they spotted the pyramidal bulk of Laramie Peak rising above the Black Hills (today's Laramie Mountains) — the first mountains seen by westering Americans.

The next day they entered into present-day Wyoming.

RAW HIDE CREEK. This stream is supposedly named from the skinning alive of a white man who shot and killed a nursing squaw near Fort Laramie, and is located at the town of Lingle, Wyoming, fifteen miles from the Nebraska line. The same story was told of the Raw Hide Creek near Fremont, Nebraska, in 1852, by a Presbyterian missionary among the Pawnees. In his *Journal* on June 1 Clayton noted,". . . the stream we passed over is called by Grosclaude: 'The Raw Hide.'" This seems to be a rare, if not unique reference to the map Grosclaude sketched for Young while at Winter Quarters the preceding November. (See page 28.)

The "Ancient Bluff Ruins" were objects of fascination to the Pioneers, who climbed among them enroute to the West. This is the most famous of Nebraska's Mormon Trail landmarks.

Chimney Rock, the most celebrated landmark on the Oregon Trail, is on the south side of the Platte River. Photo by Gregory M. Franzwa

Rebecca Winters, a Mormon pioneer who died enroute to Utah in 1852, is buried along the Mormon Trail just east of Scottsbluff, Nebraska. Photo by Gregory M. Franzwa

12

PROMINENT POINTS AND REMARKS.	DIST. miles.	From W QRS. miles.	From C of G S L miles.
"Fort John" or Laramie ford. - - The fort lays about one and a half miles west from the river. The ford is good in low water. River 108 yards wide. (See Note 3.)	12	522	509
Steep hill to descend. - - - The descent being over rock, and very steep, makes it dangerous to wagons, but it is not lengthy.	7¼	529¼	501¾
Steep hill to ascend and descend. - In traveling over this hill, you will find the road rocky in places, and about half way over there is a sudden turn in the road over rough rocks, which is dangerous to wagons, if care is not taken.	4½	533¾	497¼
Road leaves the river. - - - At this point, the road bends to the south-west, leaving the river. You will not come to the river banks again for eighty miles.	¾	534½	496½
"Warm Springs," Lat. 42° 15′ 6″. - This is a very strong spring of clear water, but it is warmer than river water, at all seasons of the year	1¾	536¼	494¾
Very steep bluff, half a mile up. - - Before arriving at this, you pass through a narrow ravine, between bluffs. The ascent is unpleasant, on account of cobble stones.	1¼	537½	493½
"Porter's Rock," left of the road. - A mile beyond this, you descend to the lower land again. The descent is steep, lengthy and sandy.	4¾	542¼	488¾
Bitter Creek and Cold Spring. - - This was dry, September 13. Here is plenty of timber, and if there is no water, you will find plenty three and a half miles further.	4¼	546½	484½
Bitter Creek—second crossing. - -	¾	547¼	483¾
Bend in the road. - - - - Road turns south about two hundred yards, to avoid a deep ravine, then back again the same distance.	2	549¼	481¾
Dead Timber creek, 10 feet wide. - Plenty of timber, grass and water.	¾	550	481
Creek, south side the road. - - You don't cross this creek, but go just above it. It is a good chance to camp.	1½	551½	479½
Small creek and spring: Lat. 42° 21′ 51″ Not safe to depend on for a camping place. Little grass and not much water—dry, September 13, 1847.	7¾	559¼	471¾
Steep hill, quarter mile up. - - Pleasant view of the surrounding country from the summit. The descent steep in several places, and many cobble stones in the road.	¼	559½	471½
"Horse Creek" and Heber's Spring. - The spring lays a little to the right of the road, at the edge of timber. If it is dry, there is water in the creek, about one hundred yards north from this spring.	5½	565	466
Bluff ¾ths of a mile to the summit. - Difficult to ascend on account of six or seven steep places, where you will probably have to double teams.	2½	567½	463½
Small creek: Lat. 42° 29′ 58″. - - After crossing this, you cross five others, about a mile apart, but none of them safe to depend on for a camping place, being little grass, and less (if any) water.	2¼	569¾	461¼

See Map Section H, Page 90

Compare *Journal,* pp. 209-224, June 2-8; pp. 361-362, Sept. 12-14.

FORT JOHN. Several forts bearing several names are known to have existed at the junction of the North Platte and Laramie Rivers. Clayton records in his *Journal* that the Pioneers forded the Platte (about 600 feet upstream from the modern highway bridge), visited the "remains of an old fort called Fort Platte . . . built about thirteen years since, and named Fort William . . . but . . . afterwards built seven years ago . . . and named John." In any event, the first structure, which came to be known as Fort Laramie, was built in 1834. The name derives from Jacques LaRamie, an early French-Canadian fur trapper who was killed by Indians about 1820. His name was then attached to a river, a mountain, a peak, a city and county, as well as to this most famous fort on the Oregon-Mormon Trail. It became a military post in 1849. See also Clayton's Note 3. At Fort Laramie the Mormons moved onto the Oregon Trail proper and followed it for some 397 miles to Fort Bridger.

STEEP HILL. This is a reference to what later became known as the famous, or infamous, "Mexican Hill," located near the Platte in Sec. 9, T26N, R65W. The Pioneers proceeded west from Fort Laramie on the "River Road," via what later came to be known as "Register Cliff" and the Warm Springs, features which were by-passed by the "Plateau or Ridge Route." See Clayton's Note 3.

STEEP HILL TO ASCEND. This is today's Deep Rut Hill near Guernsey, where the trail was worn several feet deep into solid rock, forming what may be the most dramatic trail ruts in the western hemisphere.

ROAD LEAVES THE RIVER. Here the trail leaves the easy Platte Valley and for over eighty miles proceeds as a chord to the arc of the river over relatively difficult terrain. The trail struck the Platte again about five miles east of present-day Glenrock.

WARM SPRING. These springs, which still flow, were "warm" (about 70 degrees) only in relation to the cold river. Noted by Frémont, they were also known as the "Emigrant's Washtub."

VERY STEEP BLUFF. This can be driven today in rough terrain vehicles.

PORTER'S ROCK. Here the trail split and ruts can be seen on both sides of this twelve-foot-high rock. Of no real importance, it is known today chiefly because it was supposedly named after Orrin

Porter Rockwell, frontiersman *extraordinaire* and onetime body-guard to Joseph Smith. It is in Sec. 27, T27N, R67W.

BITTER CREEK. This is today's Bitter Cottonwood Creek. It appeared on the Frémont-Preuss map as the *Fourche Amère* (Poplar Fork).

STEEP HILL. This hill is probably part of Table Mountain.

HORSE CREEK. This was originally the *Fer-à-Cheval,* or Horse-shoe Creek. These famous springs still flow and are in Sec. 7, T28N, R69W. Mormons referred to them as "Heber's Spring" because Heber C. Kimball was the first Mormon to see them. Locally they are often referred to as "Mormon Springs."

The adobe "Fort John," was painted by William H. Jackson in 1937, nearly 90 years after its demise.

The editor stands in ruts cut into solid rock by the covered wagons. The cut, nicknamed "Deep Rut Hill," is southwest of Guernsey, Wyoming. It is four feet deep in places.

"Porter's Rock" is believed to have been named for one of the Pioneers, Orrin Porter Rockwell. The trail split to go around the rock on either side; the ruts remain. Laramie Peak is in the background.

[13]

PROMINENT POINTS AND REMARKS	DIST. miles.	From W QRS. miles.	From C of G S L miles.
5th small creek from the last. - - - After crossing this, you ascend a high bluff, the top of which is a succession of hills and hollows for five miles. The road is good, but crooked.	4¾	574½	456½
"La Bonte" river, 30 feet wide, 2 ft. deep. Good place to camp—plenty of timber, grass, and water. There is also a good chance, a mile further. Plenty of wild mint on the creek.	8¼	582¾	448¼
Branch of La Bonte, 10 feet wide, 18 inches deep. - - . - - Doubtful about water. Steep banks. You have now traveled near a mile over this dark, red sand, and will find it continue three and a half miles further.	5	587¾	443¼
Very small creek. - - - - Little chance for grass, and less for water. One mile beyond this, you ascend another bluff, but the road is tolerably straight and good. Look out for toads with horns and tails.	6¼	594	437
Very small creek. - - - - Very poor chance for camping.	6¼	600¼	430¾
Very small creek. - - - - The road runs down the channel of this creek, near two hundred yards, but there is little grass on it.	½	600¾	430¼
A La Prele river, one rod wide, 2 ft. deep. Current rapid—good place to camp. Land between creeks mostly sandy and barren. Road from here to the Platte very uneven, being a succession of hills and hollows.	1½	602¼	428¾
Small creek. - - - - - - No place to camp—doubtful for water.	4¼	606½	424½
Box Elder creek, 5 feet wide. - - Clear water, and plenty—but not much grass. Not very good to cross, banks being steep. Some timber on it.	1	607½	423½
Fourche Boise river, 30 feet wide, 2 feet. deep: Lat. 42° 51′ 5″. - - Current rapid. Plenty of good grass and timber.	3¼	610¾	420¼
North fork of Platte river. - - - Not much grass here. You will now find a sandy road and heavy traveling.	4	614¾	416¼
"Deer Creek," 30 feet wide, two feet deep: Lat. 42° 52′ 50″: Altitude, 4,864 feet Lovely place to camp. Swift current, clear water, and abundance of fish. Nice grove of timber on the banks, and a coal mine about a quarter of a mile up. on the east side. After this, you will find sandy roads for nine miles, but not much grass.	5	619¾	411¼
Deep hollow, or ravine—steep banks. -	2½	622¼	408¾
Sudden bend in the road. - - - To avoid a deep ravine.	5¾	628	403
Grove of timber on the banks of the river. Good chance to camp. Lat. 42° 51′ 47″.	1	629	402
Crooked, muddy creek, 12 ft. wide, 1 deep. Not good to cross—steep banks. Plenty of grass, but no wood.	1	630	401
Muddy creek, 3 feet wide. - - - Soft banks and bad to cross. Considerable small timber, but little grass. After this, good but crooked road.	5¾	635¾	395¼
Deep gulf. - - - - -	2¾	638½	392½

See Map Section I, Page 90

Compare *Journal,* pp. 224-233, June 8-11; pp. 360-361, Sept. 9-11.

LA BONTE RIVER. This was Frémont's *R[iviere] La Bonté,* which translates as something like the benevolent river.

A LA PRELE. This was Frémont's *R. a la Prèle,* or River at the Horsetail. The horsetail is a rush-like plant useful as fodder.

BOX ELDER CREEK. Today this is called Little Box Elder Creek.

FOURCHE BOISE RIVER. This was Frémont's *F[ourche] Boisée,* or the Wooded Fork of the River, and was the farthest west either Frémont or Clayton referred to French toponyms. Today it is called Box Elder Creek.

NORTH FORK. Here the Pioneers again reached the Platte River.

DEER CREEK. This stream runs through today's Glenrock. The Mormons were interested in the vein of coal to supplement their scanty wood resources. On the return trip Young and Kimball were chased by a grizzly bear while scouting for this coal. There is a ''Mormon Canyon'' south of Glenrock.

CROOKED MUDDY CREEK. This is Muddy Creek and is just west of today's Big Muddy Oil Field.

MUDDY CREEK. This is probably today's Dry Muddy Creek.

This escarpment is above Deer Creek, near Glenrock, Wyoming. It was here that Brigham Young, Heber C. Kimball and others encountered a mother grizzly bear on their return to Winter Quarters in 1847. They escaped only by clambering up these rocky banks to safety.

14

PROMINENT POINTS AND REMARKS.	Dist. miles.	From W Qrs. miles	From C of G S L miles.
Creek, two feet wide. - - -	1½	640	391
No place to camp.			
Muddy creek, 5 feet wide, 1½ feet deep.	1	641	390
No chance to camp.			
2 ravines, near together : Lat. 42° 51′44″.	3	644	387
Opposite here there is a fording place, where companies generally have forded the river.			
Creek five feet wide. - - -	3	647	384
Abundance of fish, early in the season, but little grass, and no timber.			
Upper Platte ferry and ford. - -	1½	648½	382½
Plenty of feed and some timber on both sides the river (See Note 4.) Lat. 42° 50′ 18″. Altitude 4,875 feet.			
Road turns south, and rises a long hill. -	7	655½	375½
Ascent gradual. Many singular looking rocks on the south side. Descent rough and crooked. Towards the foot, road very uneven.			
Mineral spring and lake. - - -	5½	661	370
Considered poisonous. No bad taste to the water, unless the cattle trample in it. In that case it becomes black, and is doubtless poisonous. No timber near.			
Rock avenue and steep descent. - -	7½	668½	362½
The road here passes between high rocks, forming r kind of avenue or gateway, for a quarter of a mile.			
Alkali swamps and springs. . - -	2	670½	360½
This ought to be avoided as a camping ground—it is a small valley, surrounded by high bluffs. The land exceeding miry, and smells bad. There is a creek of good water north-west. No timber and little grass. Next mile, rough road.			
Small stream of clear spring water. -	4	674½	356½
Good camping place. Plenty of grass, but no wood.			
" Willow Spring." - - - -	2¾	677¼	353¾
About three rods west of the road, at the foot of willow bushes. Water cold and good—grass plenty, but creek some miry.			
" Prospect Hill," (summit.) - -	1	678¼	352¾
Pleasant view of the surrounding country, to the Sweet Water mountains.			
Bad slough. - - - - -	3¼	681½	349½
Plenty of grass, but little water. A mile further is a hill, both steep ascending and descending.			
Creek, 300 yards south of road. - ⌐	1¾	683¼	347¾
Plenty of grass, but no wood.			
Small creek, left of the road. . -	2½	685¾	345¼
Grass plentiful, but doubtful for water, and no wood The road runs alongside this creek for half a mile.			
Grease-wood creek, 6 feet wide 1 ft. deep.	1¾	687½	343½
Very little grass, and no fuel but wild sage. Road from here to the Sweet Water sandy, and very heavy.			
Alkali springs and lakes. - - -	6¼	693¾	337¼
Here gather your Salerætus from a lake, west of the road. Land swampy, and smells bad. Water poisonous.			
" Sweet-water river," 8 rods wide, 2 ft. deep. - - - - -	4¼	698	333
Swift current—good water. Grass plentiful, but little timber. (See Note 5)			

See Map Section J, Page 90

Compare *Journal,* pp. 233-251, June 12-21; pp. 358-360, Sept. 6-8.

MUDDY CREEK. This is a branch of the Muddy, perhaps today's Elkhorn Creek.

2 RAVINES. This ford would have been in the area where John Richard (Reshaw) later built a bridge.

UPPER PLATTE FERRY. The original Pioneer ford where the Mormons established a ferry was near present-day restored Fort Caspar (founded in 1858). Since this was where the Mormons and the trail left the Platte and its gentle valley permanently, it came to be known as Last Crossing. A later ferry was set up by the Mormons about four miles downstream in Sec. 34, T34N, R97W.

ROAD TURNS SOUTH. This refers to the ascent up today's Emigrant Gap, one of several such gaps along the trail. The Pioneers did not use the Red Buttes ford. From here west the trail went through increasingly rough and mountainous terrain.

MINERAL SPRING. There was much bad water, poor feed, and few good campsites along this stretch of the trail until they reached the Sweetwater River, some fifty miles west. It was in this area where the celebrated ox of a Mormon widow in an 1848 company collapsed, then recovered only after it had ''received a blessing.''

ROCK AVENUE. This famous rock formation runs at right angles to the trail and sometimes was called the Devil's Backbone. It is in Sec. 16, T32N, R82W. Much of it has been blasted away in recent years by highway builders.

ALKALI SWAMPS. This is more evidence of bad water along the way.

WILLOW SPRING. This was one of the few good water sources along this dreadful stretch of the trail. It still flows.

PROSPECT HILL. Now known as Ryan Hill, its 400-foot height was a great trial to draft animals. It forms the divide between the Platte and Sweetwater drainages. From its summit may be seen almost all the route from Emigrant Gap to Independence Rock.

GREASE WOOD CREEK. This is today's Horse Creek.

ALKALI SPRINGS. These are now part of the Pathfinder National Wildlife Refuge. Saleratus, or *sal aeratus,* was a raw form of sodium bicarbonate (baking soda) used by westerning Americans.

SWEET WATER RIVER. This toponym may derive from an Indian name, from the stream's contrast with the brackish water elsewhere in the area, or from a popular tale that some French *voyageurs* lost a pack mule laden with sugar in its waters. Hence, the

occasional reference to the *Eau Sucrée*. This gentle beneficent
river flows in exactly the right direction for 109 miles connecting

"Rock Avenue," an obstacle on the arid stretch between present-
day Casper and the Sweetwater River, was also called *"Devil's
Backbone."*

From the top of Prospect Hill, the Pioneers could see most of the
way back to the North Platte River. The country was and still is a
study in desolation.

Last Crossing virtually with South Pass, thus enabling travelers to get to Oregon, California or Utah in a single season.

The Pioneers enountered the Sweetwater River in the left center of this photo, just before reaching the sprawling, turtle-shaped Independence Rock, "Register of the Desert."

Devil's Gate, six miles west of Independence Rock, was another famous landmark on the trail. The Sweetwater River flows through the declivity.

15

PROMINENT POINTS AND REMARKS.	Dist. miles.	From W Qas. miles.	From C of G S L miles.
Independence Rock and ford. - -	¾	698¾	332¼
On the north side of the river—about six hundred yards long, and a hundred and twenty wide, composed of hard Granite. (See Note 5.)			
Devil's Gate. - - · -	5¼	704	327
A little west from the road. The river here passes between perpendicular rocks four hundred feet high.— This is a curiosity worthy of a traveler's notice.			
Creek two feet wide. - - -	½	704½	326½
Not good to cross. The road runs near the river banks for ten miles after this.			
Creek, 6 feet wide. - - - -	½	705	326
Good to cross. Water and grass plenty, but lacks timber. You will find grass all along on the banks of the river, but very little wood.			
Deep ravine and creek. - - -	6¼	711¼	319¾
Plenty of grass and water, but no wood.			
Deep ravine and creek. - - -	¾	712	319
Doubtful for water.			
Road leaves the river : Lat. 42° 28' 25".	3	715	316
Road after this, sandy and heavy, and passes over a high bluff. Land barren for seven and a half miles. (See Note 6.)			
Alkali Lake. - - - -	½	715½	315½
On the left of the road.			
Sage creek. - - - - -	4¾	720¼	310¾
No grass. High banks. Doubtful for water, but Wild Sage plentiful. One and three-quarter miles further you arrive on the river banks again.			
Creek, three feet wide. - - -	4	724¼	306¾
Doubtful for water, but the road runs close to the river.			
High gravelly bluff. - - -	1¼	725½	305½
Left of the road, and a very good place to camp.			
Bitter-cotton-wood creek. - - -	1½	727	304
Doubtful for water and grass. Some timber on it. After this, the road leaves the river for six miles.			
Road arrives at the river. - - -	6¼	733¼	297¾
Leave the old road and ford the river. -	¼	733½	297½
By fording here, the road is shorter, and you avoid much very heavy, sandy road. Lat. 42° 31' 20".			
Road turns between the rocky ridges. -	1½	735	296
After this, you ford the river twice—but it is easily forded. Then the road leaves the river again.			
Ford No. 4—good camping place. -	8	743	288
After this, the road leaves the river again, and you will probably find no water fit to drink for sixteen and a half miles.			
Ice Spring. - - - - -	5¾	748¾	282¼
This is on a low, swampy spot of land on the right of the road. Ice may generally be found, by digging down about two feet. There are two alkali lakes a little further.			
Alkali springs. - - - -	¼	749	282
On the left of the road			
Steep descent from the bluffs. - -	9½	758½	272½
Ford of Sweet-water, No. 5. - -	1	759½	271½
Plenty of good grass and willow bushes. River about three rods wide, and two feet deep.			

See Map Section K, Page 90-91

Compare *Journal,* pp. 252-263, June 21-25; pp. 356-358, Sept. 2-5.

INDEPENDENCE ROCK. One of the most famous landmarks on the trail, its name may derive from the fact some trappers in 1825 celebrated the Glorious Fourth there. Like most other emigrants, the Pioneers climbed its 128-foot height and left their names there.

DEVIL'S GATE. This is another famous Oregon Trail landmark. It is a 1,500-foot-long, earthquake-caused cleft in the Sweetwater Rocks, through which flows the Sweetwater River. Its name may stem from the notion of some early travelers that its 400-foot-high eastern portal resembled the profiles of two jinn facing one another.

ROAD LEAVES RIVER. Once again the road follows a chord to the river's arc to save travel time.

ALKALI LAKE. This is probably today's Soda Lake.

SAGE CREEK. This is probably today's Willow Creek.

BITTER-COTTONWOOD. This is probably today's Cottonwood Creek.

LEAVE THE OLD ROAD. Here Clayton is recommending the Three Crossings (of the Sweetwater) Route along the Sweetwater instead of the Deep Sand Route (through the Sweetwater Rocks) which the Pioneers used initially.

ROAD TURNS BETWEEN. This is the Three Crossings area about three miles northeast of today's Jeffrey City. Clayton seems to have noted only two of the three fords, hence his numbering of the well-known fords of the Sweetwater is off by one.

FORD NO. 4. This is actually the Fifth Crossing.

ICE SPRING. There was an Ice Spring and an Ice Slough. The distance from the ford suggests Clayton meant the Ice Slough. Here underground water, frozen in the winter and insulated by heavy peat-like turf, lasted into summer as ice.

FORD NO. 5. Properly, this is the Sixth Crossing.

16

PROMINENT POINTS AND REMARKS.	DIST. miles.	From W Qrs. miles.	From C of G S L miles.
Creek a rod wide. - - - - - Doubtful for water.	¼	759¾	271¼
Bluff or hill, 1½ miles to summit. - The ascent gradual, though steep in some places.	¼	760	271
Road joins the river, and fords it. - The river is forded here, to avoid crossing the next high, sandy ridge, making the road much better, and some shorter.	3½	763½	267½
Ford back. - - - - - -	½	764	267
River banks and stream, 25 feet wide. - This appears to be a branch of the river, running round a piece of land, about a quarter of a mile wide.	½	764½	266½
Creek, two feet wide: Lat. 42° 28′ 36″. A good cold spring, a little to the right of the road and a soft swamp just below, but it is a good place to camp	3	767½	263½
Road leaves the river. - - - Good camping place. After this, the road winds around and over a succession of hills and hollows, for three miles.	2	769½	261½
Rough, rocky ridges. - - - Dangerous to wagons, and ought to be crossed with care.	2½	772	259
Soft swamp and very small creek. - No place to camp.	3	775	256
Creek, a foot wide. - - - - -	1¾	776¾	254¼
Creek, two feet wide. - - -	¼	777	254
Strawberry creek, five feet wide. - Plenty of grass and water, and some willows. Good place to camp. There is a poplar grove about a mile below.	2	779	252
Quaking-aspen creek. - - - This rises in a small grove of timber on the south side the road, but is not safe to depend on for water.	1	780	251
Branch of Sweet-water, 2 rods wide, two feet deep. - - - - - - Good place to camp. Water good and cold. Grass and willows, plenty.	2¾	782¾	248¼
Willow creek, 8 feet wide, 2 feet deep. Good camping place for grass, water and willows. The ford is near three rods wide.	2¼	785	246
Sweet-water, 3 rods wide, 3 feet deep. Good place to camp. After traveling seven miles beyond this, and passing between the Twin mounds, you will find a good camping place a quarter of a mile north of the road.	4¾	789¾	241¼
SOUTH PASS, or summit of dividing ridge. This is the dividing ridge between the waters of the Atlantic and Pacific. Altitude, 7,085 feet.	9¾	799½	231½
Pacific creek and springs. - - - Abundance of grass any where for a mile. Good water, and plenty of Wild Sage for fuel.	3	802½	228½
Pacific creek (crossing) three feet wide: Lat. 42° 18′ 58″: Long. 108° 40′ 0″. Not good to cross Pretty good place to camp, except for wood. After you leave here you will find a good road, but very little water.	1½	804	227
Dry Sandy. - - - - - - The water brackish, and not good for cattle. Very little grass, but no wood.	9	813	218

See Map Section L, Page 91

Compare *Journal,* pp. 263-271, June 25-27; pp. 353-356, Aug. 27-Sept. 1.

ROAD JOINS RIVER. This is the Seventh Crossing.

FORD BACK. This is the Eighth Crossing, one-half mile distant.

ROAD LEAVES RIVER. Here the trail left the Sweetwater for over twenty miles to avoid the impassable Sweetwater Canyon.

ROUGH ROCKY RIDGES, These infamous layers of outcropping bedrock couldn't have been much preferable to the canyon and were barely negotiable by wagons. Today they may be crossed only in rough terrain vehicles.

STRAWBERRY CREEK. This was a favorite camping place.

SOFT SWAMP. This is probably today's McLean Meadows.

BRANCH OF SWEET WATER. This is today's Rock Creek, some eight miles southeast of Atlantic City, where at least fifteen members of Willie's (Mormon) Handcart Company froze to death in October 1856.

WILLOW CREEK. It is still there and still known by that name.

SWEET WATER. This was the ninth or last crossing of the Sweetwater at today's Burnt Ranch. Here emigrants left the friendly Sweetwater permanently. The Twin Mounds are located in Sections 2 and 3, T27N, R101W.

SOUTH PASS. Like most emigrants, the Pioneers could hardly discern this very gently sloped pass over the Continental Divide, which is sometimes called the "Cumberland Gap" of the West. Oregon was considered to commence immediately west of this pass. Its true height is 7550 feet. It was discovered in 1812, rediscovered in 1824, and Captain Bonneville took the first wagons over it in 1832.

PACIFIC CREEK. These famous springs, so named because their water flowed west to the Pacific Ocean, still live, forming a green oasis in a bleak area. It was a noted campsite on the trail. The longitude reading is off by seventeen minutes, or fourteen and one-half miles to the east.

DRY SANDY. This was the first stream reached after Pacific Springs.

17

PROMINENT POINTS AND REMARKS.	DIST. miles.	From W. Qrs miles.	From C of G S L miles.
Junction of California and Oregon roads. Take the left hand road. Good road a few miles, afterwards sandy and heavy.	6	819	212
Little Sandy, 20 feet wide, 2½ feet deep. Muddy water—swift current. Plenty of willows and wild sage. Abundance of grass down the stream. After this, barren and sandy land.	7¾	826¾	204¼
Big Sandy, 7 rods wide, 2 feet deep: Lat. 42° 6′ 42″. - - - - - Good chance to camp. A few miles further, you will find a short piece of rough road, over rocks and cobble stones. No grass or water after this for near 17 miles.	8¼	835	196
Big Sandy. - - - - - - Good chance to camp. After this, barren, sandy land and heavy road till you arrive at Green river.	17	852	179
Green river ford, 16 rods wide. - - Good camping any where on the banks, and plenty of timber. It is not difficult fording in low water; but if too high to ford, the best crossing place is up stream. Latitude —2 miles above—41° 52′ 37″; Long. 109° 30′. Alt. 6,000 feet.	10	862	169
Good camping place on Green river. - Plenty of grass here. But no other very good chance to camp on this side the river.	1½	863½	167½
Road leaves Green river. - - - No grass nor water after this for fifteen and a half miles. Land rolling, barren—mostly sandy, and several steep places to pass.	3½	867	164
Black's fork, 6 rods wide, 2 feet deep. - Good chance to camp, and a nice place, though not much timber.	15½	882½	148½
Ham's fork, 3 rods wide, 2 feet deep. - Rapid current, cold water, plenty of bunch grass and willows, and is a good camp ground.	3¾	886¼	144¾
Black's fork again. - - - - - Not much grass, but plenty of willows. You will now have some uneven road, with many ravines.	1¾	888	143
Small creek, 2 feet wide. - - - No grass, and probably no water.	10¾	898¾	132¼
Black's fork, third time. - - - After crossing you will find a good camping place. Plenty of bunch grass; also, wild flax.	2	900¾	130¼
Black's fork, fourth time. - - - You ford again at a good camping place.	2¼	903	128
Stream 2 rods wide, 2 feet deep. - Very swift current, and plenty of bunch grass. Road pretty rough after this.	2¾	905¾	125¼
Stream—good camping place at a bend. You do not cross the stream, but there is a good camping place, where the road passes a bend of the creek.	3½	909¼	121¾
"Fort Bridger:" Lat. 41° 19′ 13″; Long. 110° 5′; Altitude, 6,665 feet. You cross four rushing creeks, within half a mile, before you reach the Fort, and by traveling half a mile beyond the Fort, you will cross three others, and then find a good place to camp. The Fort is composed of four log houses and a small enclosure for horses. Land exceeding rich—water cold and good, and considerable timber	8¼	917½	113½

2

See Map Section M, Page 91

Compare *Journal,* pp. 272-286, June 28-July 8; pp. 351-357, Aug. 23-27.

JUNCTION. This refers to the Parting of the Ways, or the beginning of the Sublette Cutoff, which was a shortcut straight west to the Bear River.

LITTLE SANDY. It was here, northeast of present Farson, where the Pioneers met Jim Bridger.

BIG SANDY. This stream was crossed at present-day Farson and followed for seventeen miles until it was intersected again but not crossed. Southeast of this intersection are five small land features known today as the Mormon Knolls. The "barren, sandy land and heavy roads" is a reference to what is now known as the Little Colorado Desert.

GREEN RIVER FORD. Some sources refer to this river by its Shoshone name of Seedskadee (Prairie Hen) River. If Pratt's latitude reading of "41 deg. 52 min. 37 sec." is correct, this ford was at the western end of the Little Colorado Desert in Sec. 18, T22N, R109W. The longitude reading is off by sixteen minutes or over thirteen miles to the east. Later another "Mormon Ferry" was established upstream at Sec. 33, T26N, R112W. This desert is called after the Spanish name for the Green River, the *Colorado* (red or ruddy colored).

BLACKS FORK. This water source was reached at present-day Granger. The Pioneers crossed it four times before reaching Fort Bridger.

HAM'S FORK. Granger is at the confluence of Ham's Fork and Black's Fork.

FORT BRIDGER. Built in 1843 by Bridger and Louis Vasquez, this fort became an important stopping place on the trail. It was bought by the Mormons in 1855 and burned by them during the "Mormon War" of 1857. Here the Oregon Trail turned north. The Pioneers continued west along the year-old Hastings Cutoff. The longitude reading is off by fifteen minutes, or about thirteen miles to the east.

18

PROMINENT POINTS AND REMARKS.	DIST. miles.	From W QRS. miles.	From C of G S L miles.
Cold Springs, on the right side the road. There is timber here, and it is a pretty good camping place.	6¼	923¾	107¼
Small creek and springs. - - - No feed here, and no place to camp.	1¼	925	106
Summit of High Ridge: Lat. 41° 16′ 11″. After this, you travel several miles on tolerably level land, then you descend to lower land by a steep, tedious route.	1	926	105
Muddy Fork, 12 feet wide. - - Plenty of bunch grass and willows. Water clear, and not bad tasted. After this, you will probably find no good water for eleven miles.	4½	930½	100½
Copperas, or Soda Spring. - - - Left of the road at the foot of a hill. The road now begins to ascend another high ridge.	3¾	934¼	96¾
Summit of Ridge: Altitude 7,315 feet. The descent is lengthy, and some tedious. About half way down you pass over rough rocks, and the pass being narrow, makes it dangerous to wagons.	1¾	936	95
Copperas, or Soda Spring. - - - Cattle will drink this water, and there is plenty of grass around it. A little further the road turns to the left and passes down a narrow ravine.	1	937	94
Spring of good water, south side the road. This is surrounded by high grass, close to the creek side. There is another spring a little further on the north side the road, which will probably be the last water you will find till you arrive at Sulphur creek.	4½	941½	89½
East foot of dividing ridge. - - - Dividing ridge between the waters of the Colorado and Great Basin. Ascent very steep and crooked—narrow summit and steep descending. After this, crooked road between mountains. Altitude of ridge, 7,700 feet.	1	942½	88½
Sulphur creek, 10 feet wide. - - Plenty of grass and some willows; also, small cedar at the foot of the mountain. (See Note 7.)	6	948½	82½
Bear river, 6 rods wide, 2 feet deep. - Swift current—clear cold water; plenty of timber and grass. Altitude at ford, 6,836 feet.	1¾	950¼	80¾
Summit of Ridge. - - - - - Half a mile further you cross a small ridge, then descend into, and travel down a nice narrow bottom, where is plenty of grass.	2¾	953	78
Spring of clear, cold water. - - On the south side the creek. about two rods from the road. The spring is deep—water clear, cold and good. Perhaps it will not be easy to find, being surrounded by high grass.	1¾	954¾	76¼
Yellow creek, cross at foot of rocky bluffs. You will soon cross this again, and about a mile further you ascend another long ridge, the ascent being pretty steep and tedious.	4¾	959½	71½
Summit of Ridge. - - - - - Descent pretty steep. About three-fourths of a mile down from the summit, is a spring of good cold water, on the left of the road.	1¾	961¼	69¾

See Map Section N, Page 91-92

Compare *Journal*, pp. 286-291, July 8-12; p. 351, Aug. 21-22.

SUMMIT OF HIGH RIDGE. This is probably Bigelow's Bench, south of Bridger Butte.

MUDDY FORK. The Pioneers crossed this stream north of present-day Piedmont, but later Mormons went through the future townsite.

COPPERA, OR SODA SPRING. Today there is a soda spring north of Piedmont. Copperas is ferrous sulfate, which may be used as a dye. Clayton noted in his *Journal* that the water had ''a somewhat singular effect on the mouth,'' like alum.

EAST FOOT DIVIDING RANGE. This ridge, just east of today's Altamont, is one of two used by different geographers to define the eastern boundary of the Great Basin. (The other is the crest of the Wasatch Range of the Rocky Mountains.) Frémont is credited with discovering and naming the Great Basin, considered his most significant exploring accomplishment.

SULPHUR CREEK. This strong-smelling creek runs into the Bear River. The "Tar or Oil Spring" mentioned in Clayton's Note 7 still flows. It is on private property.

CLEAR RIVER. Although Clayton noted in his *Journal* on July 12 that the Pioneers "crossed the Bear River," he quite unaccountably does not identify this famous river by name in his *Guide*.

SUMMIT OF RIDGE. Beyond this ridge lay today's Coyote Creek Canyon.

SPRING. This is in Coyote Creek Canyon, which formed the beginning of a ninety-mile-long natural highway or chain of defiles, meandering through the Wasatch Range of the Rockies and into the Valley of the Great Salt Lake.

YELLOW CREEK. This creek runs at right angles to the mouth of Coyote Creek Canyon and nearly defines the present Utah-Wyoming border. The Rocky Bluffs are today's Needles, a strange formation of conglomerate rocks known as pudding stone. It was at the base of this formation where Young became ill with tick fever on July 12, and thus could not enter the Valley of the Great Salt Lake until two days after the arrival of the vanguard.

SUMMIT OF RIDGE. This ridge is immediately across the Utah border.

19

PROMINENT POINTS AND REMARKS.	DIST. miles.	From W QRS. miles.	From C of G S L. miles.
Cache Cave and head of Echo creek: Altitude, 6,070 feet. - - - Cave in the bluffs north. Several springs along the road, before you arrive here, and one, a quarter of a mile south from the Cave. Plenty of grass, and a good place to camp.	3¾	965	66
Cold spring, on the right of the road. - This also is a good place to camp, being plenty of grass	2	967	64
Cold spring, south side the road. - - At the foot of a high hill. Good place to camp. After this, you travel down a narrow ravine, between high mountains, till you arrive at Weber river. Not much difficulty for camping down it.	2¼	969¼	61¾
Deep ravine. - - - - - - Steep on both banks. After this, you will cross Echo creek a number of times, but in no place very difficult.	1¼	970½	60½
Red fork of Weber river: Alt. 5,301 feet. There is a good camping place a mile before you arrive here. Also, almost any where on the banks of the river. Plenty of timber. The stream abounds with spotted trout.	16	986½	44½
Weber river ford, 4 rods wide, 2 ft. deep. Good to ford. Plenty of grass and timber on both sides the river.	4	990½	40½
Pratt's Pass, to avoid the Kanyon. - The Kanyon is a few miles below, where the river runs between high mountains of rocks. Some emigrants have passed through, but it is dangerous.	½	991	40
East foot of Long hill. - - - - There is a small creek descends down the hollow, up which the road is made. There are several springs near the road.	1	992	39
Bridge (over the creek.) - - - Not a bad place to camp.	2¼	994¼	36¾
Summit of Ridge. - - - - - The country west looks rough and mountainous. The descent is not pleasant, being mostly on the side hill.	2½	996¾	34¼
Small creek, left of the road. - - Good place to camp. Plenty of grass, water and willows. The road here turns north a quarter of a mile, then west, and ascends a steep hill.	1¾	998½	32½
Kanyon creek, 1 rod wide, 1 foot deep: Lat. 40° 54′ 7″. - - - - - You have to cross this creek thirteen times, besides two bad swamps. The road is dangerous to wagons, on account of dense, high bushes, trees, and short turns in the road. Good place to camp. (See Note 9.)	2¾	1001¼	29¾
Leave Kanyon creek. - - - Here you turn to the right, and begin to ascend the highest mountain you cross in the whole journey. You travel through timber, some on side hills, and cross the creek a number of times.	8	1009¼	21¾
Small spring, left of the road. - - You will probably find water in several places, but it is uncertain where, as it runs but a little way in a place, and then sinks in the earth.	3	1012¼	18¾
Summit of mountain: Altitude, 7,245 feet. You have now a view of the south part of the Valley of the Great Salt Lake. The descent is steep, lengthy, and tedious, on account of stumps in the road.	1	1013¼	17¾

See Map Section O, Page 92

Compare *Journal,* pp. 291-305, July 12-13; p. 350, Aug. 19-20.

CACHE CAVE. This cave, also known as Rock, Swallow, and Reddings' cave, was a popular place for rendezvous. It is about thirty feet long, fifteen feet deep, and about six feet high, and is covered with many names.

DEEP RAVINE. Here the Pioneers entered Echo Canyon and followed it for some twenty miles to the Weber River.

RED FORK. Here the Pioneers reached the Weber River and turned north.

WEBER RIVER FORD. This crossing was at the southern end of today's community of Henefer. Here the Pioneers, like the Reed-Donner party of 1846, left the better known route through the mountains via the canyon of the Weber River and turned west. This Weber Canyon route, known to trappers since at least 1828, cleared the mountains near present-day Ogden. Of the five 1846 companies which attempted the Hastings Cutoff from Fort Bridger, four went via the Weber. The Reed-Donner party did not. The Pioneers elected to take the less known, but shorter, Reed-Donner route rather than the Weber Route. High water in the Weber may have led to this decision.

PRATT'S PASS. This is today's Main Canyon. The "kanyon" the Pioneers wished to avoid was the Weber, and when Clayton refers to "some emigrants," he means four emigrant groups who preceded the Reed-Donner party.

SUMMIT OF RIDGE. Today this is known as the Hog's Back, a place where emigrants got their first dismaying views of the mountains through which they still had to pass. Here are to be seen the best of the very few trail ruts left in Utah.

KANYON CREEK. This is today's East Canyon Creek, and was considered by Clayton to have been "the worst piece of road on the whole journey." See his Note 9.

LEAVE KANYON CREEK. Here the Pioneers started up Little Emigration Canyon to the crest of Big Mountain.

SUMMIT OF MOUNTAIN. This ridge is the much more meaningful eastern terminus of the Great Basin. From there Mormon emigrants caught their first glimpse of their new home, their Zion. The altitude of the pass is more like 7,400 feet, higher than Clayton thought it was.

20

PROMINENT POINTS AND REMARKS.	Dist. miles.	From W Qns. miles.	From C of G S L miles.
Bridge over a deep ravine. - - -	¾	1014	17
This is dangerous to cross, and a wagon may be easily upset. The road lays through a forest of small timber, and is unpleasant traveling.			
Brown's creek and spring. - - -	¾	1014¾	16¼
Not a bad place to camp, but there is a much better one, half a mile lower down.			
Cold spring on Brown's creek. - -	2¾	1017½	13½
Within a rod of the road, on the east side, under a grove of Black Birch bushes. Good place to camp, but some miry. Good camping any where for two miles lower.			
Leave Brown's creek. - - -	1¾	1019¼	11¾
You now ascend another high mountain, by a steep and crooked road. On both sides this mountain, there are many Serviceberry bushes.			
Summit of last ridge. - - - -	1	1020¼	10¾
The descent is very steep, all the way, till you arrive on the banks of Last creek.			
Last creek. - - - - -	¾	1021	10
You cross this creek nineteen times. Several of the crossings are difficult. There are several side hills which require care in teamsters. Three camping places on it, but the road is rough.			
Mouth of the Kanyon. - - -	5	1026	5
You now enter the Valley of the Salt Lake. The road at the mouth of the Kanyon bad, and rough with stumps. Afterwards, descending and good.			
CITY OF THE GREAT SALT LAKE. -	5	1031	

The city is located within three miles of the mountains, which enclose the east side of the valley—within three miles of the Utah outlet, and twenty-two miles of the Salt Lake. The land is gradually sloping, from the mountain to within a mile of the Outlet, and is of a black, loose, sandy nature. A stream of water rushes from the mountains east of the city, and, at the upper part, it divides in two branches, both of which pass through the city to the Outlet. The water is good, and very cold, and abundance for mill purposes, or for irrigation. The air is good and pure, sweetened by the healthy breezes from the Salt Lake. The grass is rich and plentiful, and well filled with rushes, and the passes in the mountains afford abundance of good timber, mostly *balsam Fir.*

The valley is about forty miles long, and from twenty to twenty-five miles wide. It is beautifully surrounded on the west, south, and east by high mountains. Salt Lake extends from a point a little south of west, from the city, to about eighty miles north, forming the north-western boundary of the

See Map Section P, Page 92

Compare *Journal,* pp. 305-309, July 21-24; pp. 347-350, Aug. 17-18.

BRIDGE. The descent down Big Mountain was one of the longest and most difficult of the trail.

BROWN'S CREEK. This probably is today's Mountain Dell Canyon Creek.

LEAVE BROWN'S CREEK. This is the ascent up Little Mountain. Many Mormons ate the small, purple serviceberries during the hard times in early Utah.

SUMMIT OF LAST RIDGE. This is the ridge of Little Mountain. Last Creek is today's Emigration Canyon Creek.

MOUTH OF THE KANYON. Even with the initial work of road making by the Reed-Donner party, it took the Pioneers sixteen days and ten camps to traverse the 116 miles from Fort Bridger to the valley. About one mile from the mouth of the canyon the Reed-Donner party gave up hacking out a road and forced their animals up Donner Hill, thereby jading their draft teams and leaving the Mormons one mile of trail to blaze. This was the most important of the very few miles of trail which Mormons ever initiated. Whenever possible, in all their moving around, they used the best roads available and avoided making their own.

The Pioneers caught this first view of the Valley, their Zion, from Big Mountain.

21

valley. There are two sulphur springs a mile and a half north from the *TEMPLE BLOCK; the water is salt, and a little warmer than blood: two miles further north there is a sulphur spring of boiling water. There is not much land on the north part of the valley fit for cultivation; but the east side is well adapted for farming, being well watered by several large creeks, and the soil beautiful. The land on the west of the Utah Outlet, is also good for farming, and easily irrigated from the south end of the Outlet.

The latitudes, longitudes, and altitudes are copied from the observations and calculations made by Elder O. PRATT.

The variation of the magnetic needle, at the City of the Great Salt Lake, 15° 47′ 23″ east, as determined on the 30th July, A. D. 1847, by the mean of several observations, and calculations of the Sun's Azimuths and Altitudes.

---

* Latitude of northern boundary of Temple Block, 40° 45′ 44″.
    Longitude of do.   do.   do.   111° 26′ 34″.
    Altitude of   do.   do.   do.   4,300 feet.

22

NOTES.

NOTE I. If the Elk Horn river is fordable, you leave the main road a mile before you strike the river, and turn north. After leaving the road *three-fourths* of a mile, you will cross a very bad creek or slough, being soft and miry; but, by throwing in long grass, it will be good crossing. You then travel three-fourths of a mile further, and arrive at the ford. You will go up stream when fording, and gradually come nearer to the opposite shore, till you strike a piece of low land on the west side; you then pass by a narrow, crooked road, through the timber, till you arrive on the open prairie. You will then see a *post* erected in near a south direction, about a mile distant. Go straight to that post, and you will find a good bridge over the creek—and there, again strike the main road. From here, you have before you near five hundred miles travel over a flat, level country, and a good road, with the exception of several sandy bluffs mentioned herein. The road generally runs from one to two miles from the Platte river, but not too far to turn off to camp in case of necessity. All camping places, which lay near the road, are mentioned in this work. You will find near two hundred miles without timber, but in that region you will find plenty of buffalo chips, which are a good substitute for fuel. Buffalo are numerous after you arrive at the head of Grand Island, and continue two hundred miles.

NOTE II. The descent to the ford is steep, and at the bottom very sandy. Your best chance to ford will, probably, be to enter the river opposite to where you descend from the bluff; then go near a straight course, but inclining a little down stream, till more than half way over, when you will find a sand-bar. Follow this, down stream near half a mile, and you will then see a good place to go out on the south side. In this river the channels often change—the old ones fill up, and new ones are made—hence, the wisdom and necessity of having several men go across on horses, to find the best route, before you attempt to take wagons over. If this precaution is not taken, you may plunge your wagons from a sand-bar into a deep hole, and do much damage. If you ford up stream, and come out higher than where you enter, after crossing, strike for the bluffs, in a direction a very little west of south, till you arrive on the old road.

On arriving at Prairie creek, if you take a south-west course, a short day's drive will bring you to Wood river, six or eight miles above where the old road crosses; and by keeping the same course after crossing Wood river, you will strike

23

the Platte ten or twelve miles above where Wood river empties into it. By this means the road would be shortened at least five miles, and probably much more.

Note iii. Fort "John, or Laramie," lays about one and a half miles from the river, in near a south-west course, and is composed of a trading establishment, and about twelve houses, enclosed by a wall eleven feet high. The wall and houses are built of *adobes*, or Spanish brick. It is situated on the Laramie Fork, and is a pleasant location: the latitude of the Fort is 42° 12' 13"; longitude 104° 11' 53", and altitude above the sea, 4,090 feet. After leaving here you begin to cross the "Black Hills," and will find rough roads, high ridges, and mostly barren country. There is, however, not much difficulty in finding good camping places, each day's travel, by observing the annexed table.

There is a road follows the river, instead of crossing the Black Hills, and it is represented as being as near, and much better traveling if the river is fordable. By following this road you have to cross the river three times extra, but will find plenty of grass, wood, and water. If the river is fordable at Laramie, it is fordable at those three places, and you can go that route safely.

Note iv. The best place to ford will probably be a little below the bend in the river. After this you have fifty miles to travel, which is dangerous to teams, on account of Alkali springs. Great care should be taken to avoid them, by selecting a camping place where none of these springs are near.

Note v. In low water the river is easily forded opposite to the Rock Independence; but, if not fordable here, a good place can be found a mile higher up the river.

Independence Rock is one of the curiosities to be seen on the road, mostly on account of its peculiar shape and magnitude. There are many names of visitors painted in various places, on the south-east corner. At this corner most travelers appear to have gone up to view the top; but there is a much better place on the north side, about half way from end to end. Latitude 1½ miles below 42° 30' 16".

The road along the Sweet Water is mostly sandy and heavy traveling. You will find many steep places, and as you approach the Rocky Mountains, you will find some high hills to travel over.

After crossing the mountains the country is level, but still barren, and, if possible, more sandy. You will have to make some long drives to obtain water for camping. There is great lack of timber, from the Upper Platte ferry to Fort Bridger,

24

and in fact scarcely any kind but willows. In all this region the willows and wild sage form your chief ingredient for fuel.

NOTE VI. It is supposed that a good road can be made here, by following the banks of the river. If so, these high bluffs, and much sandy road, would be avoided.

NOTE VII. At the foot of the mountain, on the south side the road, and at the edge of the creek, there is a strong sulphur spring. A little above the spring, on the side of the moun-tain, is a bed of stone coal. At the foot of the bluff, west of where you cross the creek, is a noble spring of pure, cold water; and about a mile from this place, in a south-west course, is a "Tar," or "Oil Spring," covering a surface of several rods of ground. There is a wagon trail runs within a short distance of it. It is situated in a small hollow, on the left of the wagon trail, at a point where the trail rises a higher bench of land.

When the oil can be obtained free from sand, it is useful to oil wagons. It gives a nice polish to gun-stocks, and has been proved to be highly beneficial when applied to sores on horses, cattle, &c.

NOTE VIII. From the summit of this ridge, you will see to the west, a ridge of high, rough, peaked rocks. The road runs at the south foot of that ridge, and there crosses Yellow creek. From the place where you now stand, the road runs through a beautiful narrow valley, surrounded by gently rolling hills, and is pretty straight and pleasant traveling, till you ar-rive at that ridge of rocks. There is little difficulty in finding a good camping place, between here and the ridge in view, ex-cept for fuel, which is scarce. There are several springs of good water along the creek.

NOTE IX. On this creek is a very rough piece of road; the bushes are high, and road narrow, in consequence of which wagon covers are liable to be torn, and bows broke. There are many short turns in it, where wagon tongues are liable to be broke. Some of the crossing places are bad. There is a good camping place where first you strike the creek—one about half way up, and one a quarter of a mile before you leave the creek.

The ascent up the next mountain is both lengthy and tedi-ous, mostly through high timber, and there are many stumps in the road. It is a chance whether you will find any water till you descend on the west side.

From this creek to the valley is decidedly the worst piece of road on the whole journey, but the distance is short, and by using care and patience, it is easily accomplished.

The trail down Coyote Creek Canyon, toward Utah, was easy to negotiate. The formation in the background, "The Needles," is where Brigham Young came down with a severe attack of mountain fever, delaying his entry into the Valley.

CONTEMPORARY MAPS

These maps have been taken from *Discovering Mormon Trails,* Deseret Book Co., 1979. Reprinted by permission.

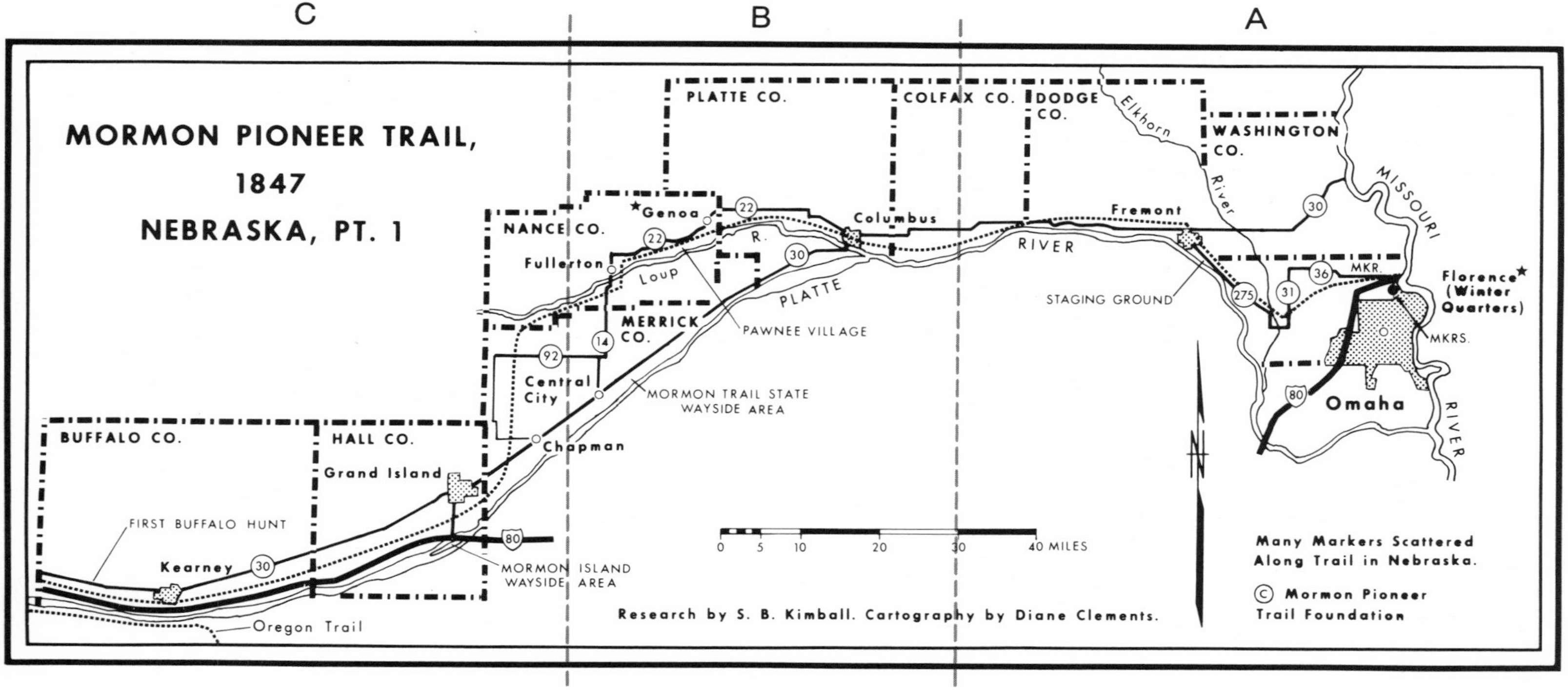

MORMON PIONEER TRAIL,
1847
NEBRASKA, PT. 1

Research by S. B. Kimball. Cartography by Diane Clements.

Many Markers Scattered
Along Trail in Nebraska.

Ⓒ Mormon Pioneer
Trail Foundation

0 5 10 20 30 40 MILES

MISSOURI   RIVER
Florence★
(Winter
Quarters)
MKRS.
MKR
Omaha
36
31
275
80

WASHINGTON CO.
Elkhorn River
30
Fremont
STAGING GROUND
DODGE CO.
COLFAX CO.
PLATTE CO.
Columbus
PLATTE   RIVER
30
22
Loup R.
22
Genoa★
NANCE CO.
Fullerton
14
MERRICK CO.
PAWNEE VILLAGE
MORMON TRAIL STATE
WAYSIDE AREA
92
Central City
Chapman
80
MORMON ISLAND
WAYSIDE AREA
HALL CO.
Grand Island
BUFFALO CO.
30
Oregon Trail
FIRST BUFFALO HUNT
Kearney

A   B   C

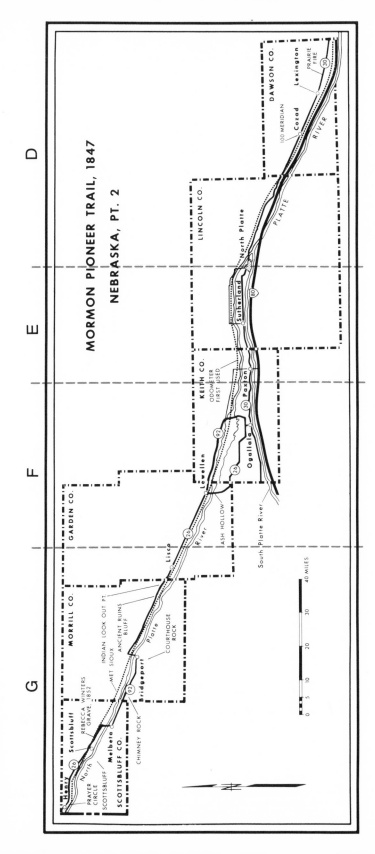

MORMON PIONEER TRAIL, 1847
NEBRASKA, PT. 2

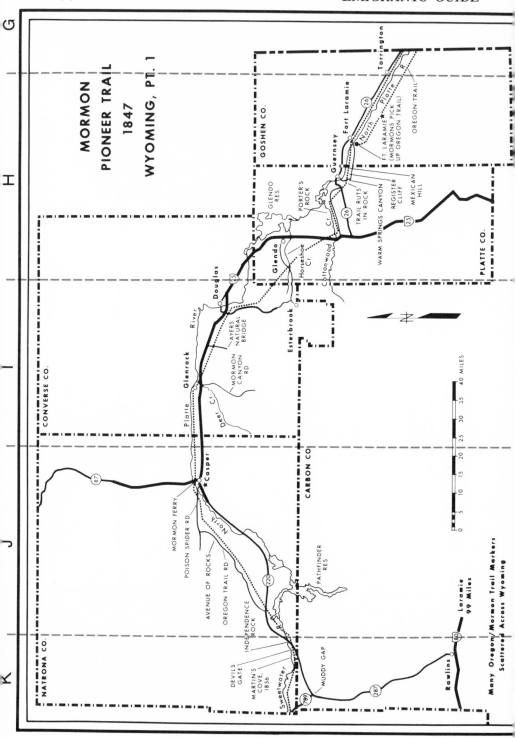

MORMON
PIONEER TRAIL
1847
WYOMING, PT. 1

GOSHEN CO.

Torrington

Fort Laramie
Guernsey
26
North Platte
R.
FT. LARAMIE
(MORMONS PICK
UP OREGON TRAIL)
OREGON TRAIL

GLENDO
RES.
PORTER'S
ROCK
TRAIL RUTS
IN ROCK
REGISTER
CLIFF
MEXICAN
HILL
WARM SPRINGS CANYON
25

PLATTE CO.

Douglas
45
Glendo
Horseshoe Cr.
Cottonwood Cr.

26

CONVERSE CO.

Glenrock
Platte River
AYERS
NATURAL
BRIDGE
MORMON
CANYON
RD.
Deer Cr.
Esterbrook

N

CARBON CO.

Casper
87
MORMON FERRY
POISON SPIDER RD.
North Platte R.
AVENUE OF ROCKS
OREGON TRAIL RD.
220
PATHFINDER
RES.

0 5 10 15 20 25 30 35 40 MILES

NATRONA CO.

INDEPENDENCE
ROCK
DEVILS
GATE
MARTIN'S
COVE,
1856
Sweetwater R.
MUDDY GAP
789

287
Rawlins
80
Laramie
99 Miles

Many Oregon/Mormon Trail Markers
Scattered Across Wyoming

G H I J K

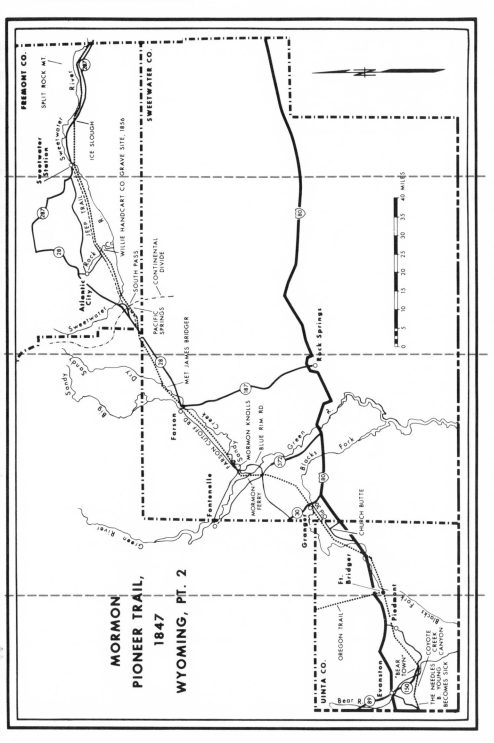

MORMON
PIONEER TRAIL,
1847
WYOMING, PT. 2

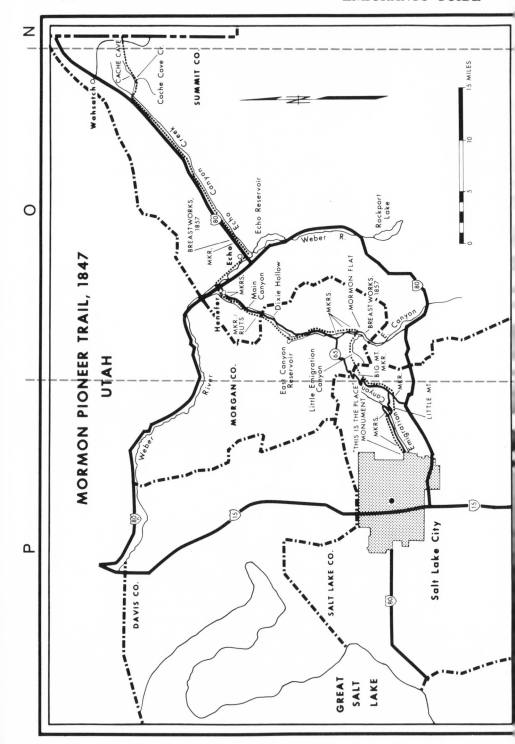

MORMON PIONEER TRAIL, 1847
UTAH

HISTORICAL MAPS

Overleaf:
THE 1823 MAP OF MAJ. S.H. LONG: This was considered the best map of the Platte River Valley until the Frémont-Preuss maps of 1843-1845 and 1846. It is presumed the Pioneers were familiar with this map.

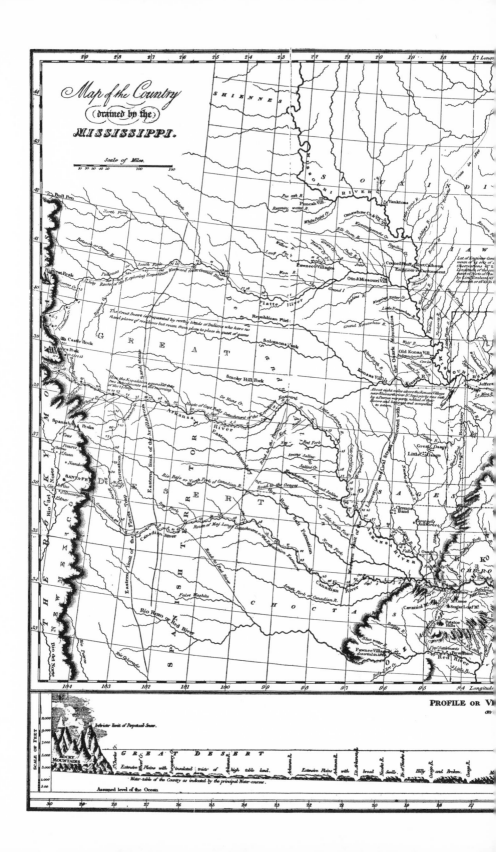

Map of the Country
(drained by the)
MISSISSIPPI.

Scale of Miles.

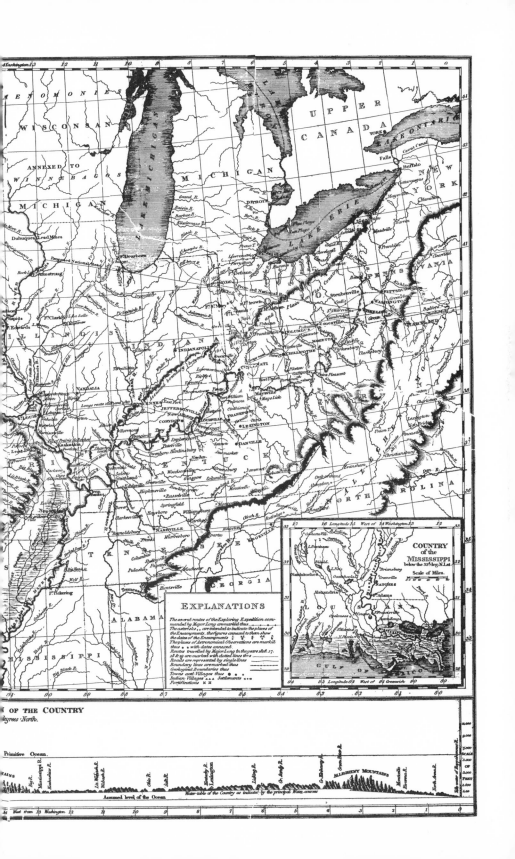

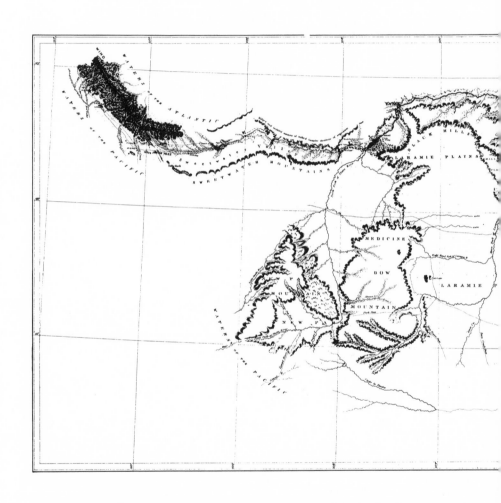

THE FRÉMONT-PREUSS MAP OF 1843: This is the famous map
Stephen A. Douglas sent from Washington D.C. to Joseph Smith,

the map the Pioneers consulted in Nauvoo, took west with them, and
which Clayton referred to so often. The Platte River is shown in
blue on the original.

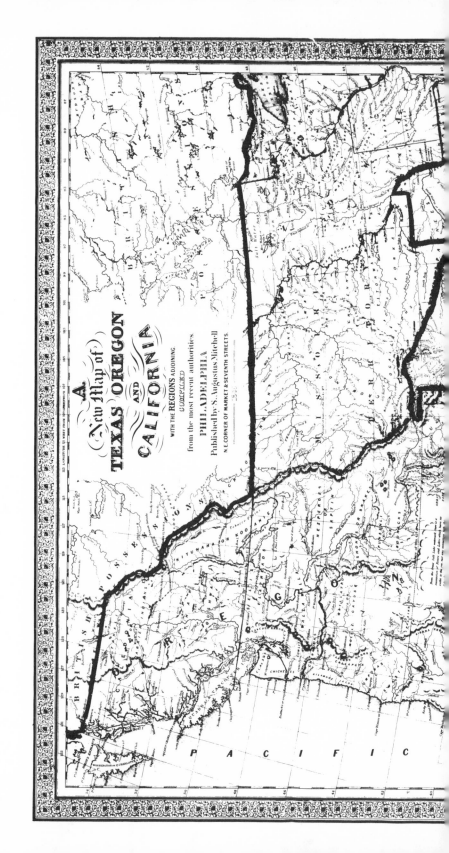

A New Map of TEXAS OREGON AND CALIFORNIA WITH THE REGIONS ADJOINING. COMPILED from the most recent authorities PHILADELPHIA Published by S. Augustus Mitchell N.E. CORNER OF MARKET & SEVENTH STREETS

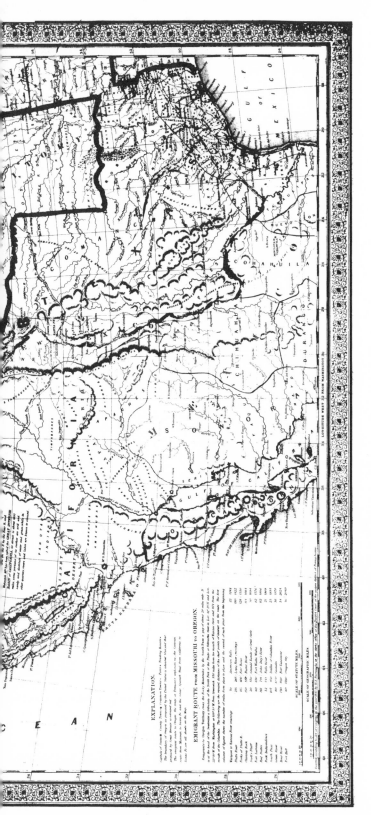

MITCHELL'S 1846 MAP: In 1846 Brigham Young specifically ordered from St. Louis a copy of this map, which the Pioneers took west. This map was hand tinted in four colors.

BILL OF THE ROUTE

MILES.

		Total.	
From INDEPENDENCE to Crossing of the Kanzas, - - -	90		This is the general estimate of the distance, to the point where emigrants usually cross this river. At the season in which companies for Oregon or California generally leave the States, there is, in this distance, every where, an abundance of wood, water, and grass. The Kanzas River is generally full in the Spring, but emigrants will probably hereafter be accommodated, by a Frenchman who resides at the crossing place, with a ferry-boat. Owing to the time required in crossing, and the consequent accumulation of great numbers of animals, the grass in this vicinity, will likely become, in a few days, insufficient.
Muddy Creek, -	17	107	From the crossing, the road leaves the river gradually to the left. Here there is an abundance of wood and grass. The creek is small but deep, and the crossing has formerly been difficult.
Honey Creek, -	20	127	In the intermediate distance, the road, which still continues to leave the Kanzas River more and more to the left, crosses, every few miles, small creeks upon which there are good camps. At Honey Creek, there is the greatest abundance of wood and grass.
A small creek, -	9	136	Upon this, there is much grass—some wood.
Another, - -	3	139	do do
Another, - -	4	143	do do
Canon-Ball Creek,	2	145	Upon Cannon-Ball Creek, there is an abundance of grass and wood.
A branch, - -	11	156	But little wood—grass abundant.
Another, - -	5	161	do do

This is the first page of a Bill of Route, or guide, from Overton Johnson and William H. Winters' popular Route Across the Rocky Mountains, *Lafayette, Ind., 1846. Clayton may have gotten the idea for the format of his* Guide *from such an example as this.*

No. 16   Come, Come, Ye Saints
W. CLAYTON

1. Come, come, ye Saints, no toil nor labor fear, But with joy wend your way;
2. Why should we mourn, or think our lot is hard? 'Tis not so; all is right!
3. We'll find the place which God for us prepared, Far a-way in the West;
4. And should we die before our journey's through, Hap-py day! all is well!

Tho' hard to you this jour-ney may appear, Grace shall be as your day.
Why should we think to earn a great re-ward, If we now shun the fight?
Where none shall come to hurt or make a-fraid; There the Saints will be blessed.
We then are free from toil and sor-row too; With the just we shall dwell.

'Tis bet-ter far for us to strive Our use-less cares from
Gird up your loins, fresh cour-age take, Our God will nev-er
We'll make the air with mu-sic ring— Shout prais-es to our
But if our lives are spared a-gain To see the Saints, their

us to drive; Do this, and joy your hearts will swell—All is well! All is well!
us for-sake; And soon we'll have this truth to tell— All is well! All is well!
God and King; Above the rest these words we'll tell—All is well! All is well!
rest ob-tain, O how we'll make this chorus swell— All is well! All is well!

"Come, Come, Ye Saints," the most famous of Mormon hymns, is often termed the "Mormon Marseillaise." Clayton wrote the words near the beginning of The Exodus, on April 15, 1846, on Locust Creek in Wayne County, Iowa. Some of the words and most of the melody were inspired by an old English song, "All Is Well."

The incredible Platte River braided its way across Nebraska and Wyoming, forming a gentle, friendly valley for both the Mormon and Oregon trails.

INDEX

Illustrations are indicated by italic numerals.

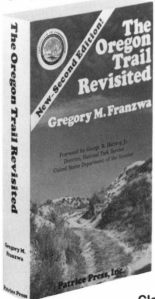

HISTORIC SITES ALONG THE OREGON TRAIL
Aubrey L. Haines

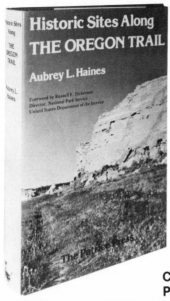

Now, in this single volume, the reader may obtain complete information on virtually all sites of historic importance along the Oregon Trail, from Independence, Mo., to Oregon City, Ore. Each site description includes the name, location (to a tolerance of 200 yards), distance from Independence, a general summation, material extracted from the journals of the 19th century emigrants, then the 20th century revisitors. Haines usually has remarks of his own to add, and closes with the name of the map on which that particular site may be found.

1983 Retail Price:
Cloth: $24.95
Mo. residents please
add $1.15 sales tax

Paper: $9.95
Mo. residents please
add 46¢ sales tax

Cloth: ISBN: 0-935284-21-4
Paper: ISBN 0-935284-28-1

Mailing, either book:
$1.75

THE WAKE OF THE PRAIRIE SCHOONER
Irene D. Paden

Irene D. Paden studied the Oregon Trail exhaustively for eight years, making her first field trips in 1935 and concluding her study in 1943 with the publication of this remarkable book. Here is a rare personal literary exposition of the trail as it appeared a half-century ago. Solid, deep and continuous ruts are described in Kansas and elsewhere, which have long since disappeared. Her observations are spiced with her family's trials and tribulations as they searched out the highlights of the old trail. They inquired of local farmers, combed county courthouse records, and studied countless diaries. This facsimile edition was published in 1969. 533 pages, index.

1983 Retail Price:
Paper only: $5.95
Mailing: $1.35
Mo residents please
add 28¢ sales tax

ISBN 8093-0462-7

The Patrice Press
1701 South Eighth Street
St. Louis MO 63104